HIDDEN HISTORY
of CIVIL WAR
SOUTH CAROLINA

D. Michael Thomas

THE
History
PRESS

Published by The History Press
Charleston, SC
www.historypress.com

First published 2025

Manufactured in the United States

ISBN 9781467158077

Library of Congress Control Number: 2024947371

Remember, Reflect, Respect and Retell to the next generation
—Author unknown

This book is dedicated to those who taught me history in high school and college. True teachers, they were able to present the past in ways that made it seem alive, real and exciting.

CONTENTS

CONTENTS

PREFACE

The North and South fought the bloodiest war in this nation's history between 1861 and 1865. Historians have recorded over 10,000 battles and skirmishes in that period resulting in the deaths of over 700,000 soldiers, sailors and marines from both sides. Further, nearly 100,000 Southern civilians, Black and White, perished as the result of this conflict, which goes by many names. Though it is commonly called the Civil War or the War Between the States, the most appropriate moniker is the War for Southern Independence.

No one knows how many books have been written on this war. Best estimates say the list is well over 100,000 and growing daily. The overwhelming majority focus on the causes of the war, strategy and command, military campaigns, the great battles and leading military or political figures. This work is not one of them.

Famed author Rudyard Kipling is credited with the quote, "If history were taught in the form of stories, it would never be forgotten." His words reflect perfectly the intentions of this book. Written to present little stories and events involving the Palmetto State and its citizen-soldiers, the fifty stories within these pages present an array of topics rarely mentioned elsewhere. While deliberately staying away from the great battles, leaders and other topics covered numerous times by others, they add greatly to the understanding of what the Palmetto State experienced on a personal and local level.

Much of our history has been lost since that terrible war ended and what remains is often ignored. South Carolinians who lived through it took much of their wartime experience and knowledge to the grave with them. Some, however, did put their roles and knowledge to pen and paper. The first decade of the twentieth century was of immense value to historians, for only then was it possible and acceptable for former Confederate servicemen to record their wartime experiences for posterity. That decade produced much of the documentation available to today's historians, scholars, authors and students. It remains invaluable, fully worthy of study and available to all who will seek it.

From my early days of study and research on this conflict, I have kept track of numerous fascinating stories and accounts involving South Carolina and its men that popped up in a variety of sources. Most were found in postwar accounts by those involved, magazines dedicated to the study of the war and period newspaper articles such as the wartime editions of the *Charleston Mercury* and *Richmond (VA) Daily Dispatch*. Books and articles published by true historians and scholars have provided others. Confirmation of these stories has been carried out through liberal use of the *Official Records* for both the armies and the navies as well as studying the compiled service records of individual servicemen. Additional sources of all sorts have been sought and found in form of several wartime diaries and a previously neglected and extremely valuable letter collection.

This collection of "golden nuggets" forms the basis for this work. Some accounts introduce soldiers long-forgotten but whose deeds should be remembered with respect. Others add critical details allowing for a clearer understanding of well-known topics, events or subjects. Some are there simply for their uniqueness. Together, they present material omitted, whether overlooked or simply ignored, over the years by most studies. Readers will quickly discover this work is a series of accounts introducing figures and events solely for the sake of adding additional depth to South Carolina's wartime history of events and of its men in service. Most will be new to students or casual readers and even many historians.

The postwar section of this work is certainly worthy of inclusion, for it provides a clear understanding of efforts by South Carolinians to gather, honor and memorialize their fallen men. Today's citizenry sees certain memorials and monuments but have no understanding of what prompted their placement. The fact that the U.S. Navy named ships with Confederate connections for decades will likely soon languish into obscurity. This work, by extension, serves to preserve and promote those stories and other deserving postwar accounts relating to South Carolina and its men under arms.

The study of military campaigns, great battles and army leaders can be likened to the meat and potatoes in learning about the war. This book can be likened to the spices used to flavor them. The material within it, history in form of topics rarely ever addressed anywhere nowadays, expands our knowledge of the larger pictures in a manner that, as Kipling suggests, will be remembered.

The material within these pages comes not from anecdotes, yarns or tales but actual accounts taken from historically reliable sources. Quite a few were truly newsworthy in their day. Unfortunately, their relevance has been lost over the years, particularly since the Centennial commemoration in the 1960s. Some raise hardly a ripple in the grand study of the war while others provide important new material and insight for study. Several are included because they were just plain interesting. Together, they present subject matter worthy of notice by history-minded folks in today's world and those of future generations.

Much effort has been expended to place each account in context to ensure clarity and a proper perspective. The topics selected for this book represent only a small portion of South Carolina's wartime history. Hopefully, readers will be inspired to conduct their own research and bring more of these little-known stories to light. I have drawn several accounts from my previous books for the articles on Wade Hampton's Iron Scouts and General Stephen Elliott, for they are the only works ever written on them. Some of the pieces herein have been previously published and are reproduced here with permission.

ACKNOWLEDGEMENTS

I owe thanks to a number of folks and institutions. My wife, DeeDee, provided the initial concept, encouragement and support provided in making this work come to fruition. I cannot overlook the endorsements given by Bill Norris and other close associates who share my love and respect for South Carolina's history.

The South Caroliniana Library of the University of South Carolina is a gold mine for researchers. The staff members there I spoke with proved in every instance to be supportive and available.

Mary Boyd of the Georgetown County Museum and Ben Burroughs at Coastal Carolina University proved most helpful in my research on blockade running in Horry and Georgetown Counties. A special acknowledgement goes to Tracy Jenzor, who shared her master's thesis on blockade running at Murrell's Inlet and Little River with me. With their help and guidance, I was able to finally see the importance and volume of the blockade-running along the usually unheralded sites of coastal South Carolina.

Finally, I am most grateful to my good friend since childhood Roger Dobbins. He contributed mightily by ensuring many of the images within this work were of the highest quality possible while, at the same time, offering encouragement and valuable, thoughtful suggestions.

1

SOUTH CAROLINA IN OVERVIEW

1861–1865

This short recapitulation of events within the state is intended to provide a backdrop and time frame for reference, perspective and understanding of the changing circumstances and conditions as the war continued. It touches on some aspects and events unmentioned by most twenty-first-century historians and authors.

Each state within the Confederacy had its own unique wartime experiences. South Carolina's involvement was unquestionably critical throughout the war. Though it saw none of the "great" battles on the scale of Gettysburg, Shiloh or Chickamauga, its ability to hold against Union assaults for nearly four years caused great frustration for Northern military commanders while uplifting defiant spirits of citizens all across the South.

South Carolina provided about seventy-five thousand men to the Confederate army. Almost twenty-five thousand died of wounds or disease during the war. Among the state's forty-six generals, four were lieutenant generals (James Longstreet, Wade Hampton III, Stephen Dill Lee and Richard H. Anderson) and several others were major generals. South Carolina's soldiers fought in North Carolina, Georgia, Maryland, Mississippi, Alabama, Tennessee and Pennsylvania as well as in their home state.

Men from the Palmetto State served honorably and bravely for Southern independence from the firing on Fort Sumter to the final surrenders at

Courtesy of David Coates.

Appomattox, Durham Station and elsewhere four years later. In between, they provided many acts of heroism that still resonate today while others, no less heroic, have faded from the public eye. Much has been written about Sergeant Richard Kirkland, who gained eternal fame as the "Angel of Marye's Heights" by administering water and aid to dozens of wounded Union soldiers following their failed assaults at Fredericksburg. Yet Captain Joseph Banks Lyle, despite capturing nearly six hundred Yankees virtually single-handedly in the 1864 Battle of Williamsburg Road, is virtually unknown. Together, the individual stories etched in the annals reflect high courage, strength of character, strong leadership and Christian principles of South Carolina's soldiers.

The first shots of the war were fired in Charleston on April 12, 1861, and the last shots fired by organized forces east of the Mississippi occurred near Williamston, South Carolina, on May 1, 1865, involving Citadel cadets. In between those dates, South Carolina saw over 150 battles and skirmishes within its borders. It should be noted that South Carolina was the only state within the Confederacy that did not provide a White regiment to the Union army.

After the capture of Fort Sumter in Charleston's harbor in April 1861, the focus of events transferred to Virginia. Freshly raised commands were rushed there to stop invasion by Union forces. Both the North and South thought the war would be ended in a single decisive battle, but the long-awaited engagement at First Manassas, a Confederate victory, simply brought the realization that the conflict would be an extended one.

War came slowly to South Carolina. The Union navy began a loose blockade of Charleston on May 28, 1861, and at Port Royal Sound shortly afterward. The following November, Port Royal Sound was captured by Northern forces. This devastating loss allowed the Union fleet to build a facility for repair, maintenance and supply of their ships blockading the South Atlantic ports. By December 1861, Georgetown was effectively blockaded, thus adding further restrictions to the shipping trade of South Carolina's major ports. Ground operations were not begun until 1862, but until January 1865, these were constrained to the coastal corridor from Port Royal Sound northward to Charleston.

The Union capture of Port Royal also posed a threat to the vital Charleston and Savannah Railroad running close to the coast. General Robert E. Lee, sent to South Carolina as commander of the Department of South Carolina, Georgia and East Florida, established and maintained his headquarters at Coosawhatchie. Serving in this capacity from early November 1861 through early March 1862, he formed and put in place a plan of defense for this railroad. The Battle of Port Royal clearly showed the overwhelming firepower of the U.S. Navy's heavy guns. Accordingly, Lee ordered erection of earthwork defensive positions at critical inland points

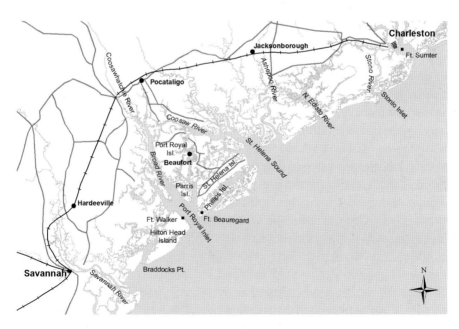

Map showing the Charleston and Savannah Railroad, a frequent target of Union forces. *Courtesy of Scott Williams.*

well away from their reach, thus depriving Union troops of their valuable support when attempting any ground offensive. Despite initial protests, Lee's plans were carried out and the results were exactly as anticipated—Union ground operations were stopped cold.

The first of several attempts to sever the railroad and isolate Charleston was near Pocotaligo on May 29, 1862. There, about 1,000 Union soldiers carrying muskets were defeated by fewer than 100 Confederate cavalrymen fighting on foot and armed only with shotguns and revolvers in an intense four-hour action. Another concerted effort to break the railroad near Beaufort was made the following October when a two-pronged Union force of 4,500 men was stopped at Pocotaligo and Coosawhatchie by fewer than 700 men in gray. Sandwiched between these two actions, Confederate forces decisively beat back a determined Union assault in the June 16 Battle of Secessionville on James Island. Had this assault been successful, it is almost certain Charleston would have fallen shortly afterward. These three stunning victories kept Confederate morale high and prompted Union generals to delay further major land operations until July 1863.

The Beaufort area remained a center of activity in 1862 with Confederate raiders harassing Union outposts. Two instances resulted in national coverage. A raid on Pinckney Island resulted in nearly all the fifty-seven Union troops there being killed or captured. In another instance, the Union army gunboat *George Washington* was ambushed and sunk by Confederate artillery.

Charleston, meanwhile, was building its defensive network in anticipation of attack by land or sea. Confederate defenses along the coast were established and troops were kept available to move by rail to any point between Charleston and Savannah threatened by Union forces. Charleston's importance grew as it became the primary port for blockade runners in the South followed closely by Wilmington, North Carolina. This status ended in September 1863 when Charleston's harbor was effectively closed for six months after the fall of Battery Wagner and Morris Island.

From April 1862 through the war's end, Union transports laden with troops and escorted by gunboats sailed into the bays and rivers all along the coast. From Port Royal to the North Carolina border, these expeditions landed at plantations to loot and pillage before destroying crops, mills, barns and houses. Many of the state's island communities were abandoned by their citizens and occupied by Union forces. Plantations along the

Santee River, Winyah Bay and all around the Beaufort area were hard-hit by these raids, and much farmland in these areas remained fallow until war's end. Still, the Yankees were confined to the coast and the inland areas remained safe.

On January 31, 1863, in early morning darkness and fog, the C.S. Navy sent the ironclad gunboats CSS *Chicora* and CSS *Palmetto State* from Charleston's harbor to break the Union blockade. They successfully damaged four wooden Union warships and drove the remainder away temporarily. The consuls of England, France and Spain at Charleston reported to their governments that the blockade was indeed broken under international law, but Lincoln's government chose to ignore these findings and continued blockading efforts. This was the only high-seas clash during the war involving Confederate ironclads.

In late February, the Union navy took another hit when Confederate batteries ambushed and captured a Union gunboat, *Isaac P. Smith*, in the Stono River near Charleston. The vessel was repaired and placed into Confederate service before conversion to a blockade runner. With Union attention firmly focused on Charleston, a major attempt to silence Forts Sumter and Moultrie with a fleet of monitors and ironclads in April was soundly defeated. In October 1863, another attempt to break the Charleston naval blockade was carried out by a small spar-torpedo boat called the *Little David*, which successfully damaged the North's most powerful warship, the USS *New Ironsides*, prompting it to be sent away for extensive repairs for several months.

In July, a revised plan to subdue Charleston calling for the capture of Morris Island and destruction of Fort Sumter by heavy artillery was initiated. However, it took fifty-nine days to take Morris Island because of the strength of Battery Wagner on Morris Island and the fortitude of those defending it. In August, heavy Union guns began firing indiscriminately into the city of Charleston and continued to do so until the city was finally taken in February 1865. Sumter was pounded and reduced to an infantry outpost by nearly twenty-seven thousand shells from August through December, including a forty-one-day bombardment (October 26–December 6) of over eighteen thousand shells. Still, Union forces failed to capture the fort or drive its garrison away, and the Confederate flag continued to wave defiantly in the sea breezes. On New Year's Eve 1863, Union general Quincy Gilmore, commanding all army troops along the coast, showed his respect and admiration for Fort Sumter's commanding officer, Lieutenant Colonel Stephen Elliott, by dipping his Cummings Point garrison flag in formal salute as Sumter's evening colors gun was fired. This unprecedented honor is without parallel in U.S. military history.

The year 1864 was one of high tension in both the North and South. Many great battles had been fought in Virginia and elsewhere, resulting in massive casualties on both sides. Destruction across the South by Union raids and occupation led to horrible depredations against Southern civilians, Black and White. Still, the issues were in doubt, and Abraham Lincoln's reelection was in great jeopardy. It was an accepted fact that Southern independence hung on the Northern ballot.

In February, the South launched a new weapon from Charleston. The spar-torpedo boat *H.L. Hunley* made the first successful submarine attack in history by sinking the USS *Housatonic* while it was blockading Charleston. Fort Sumter and other Charleston fortifications continued to receive periodic bombardments, but little else took place until July when the Union army began a series of assaults all around Charleston. Troops were landed on James Island and Johns Island but met such resistance they feared they would be overrun by Confederate forces and withdrew in a hurried manner. Other attacks elsewhere failed, including the loss of the entire landing party at Fort Johnson. Fort Sumter was subjected to a sixty-day bombardment (July 7–September 4) in which another 14,600 heavy shells were fired at it. When these efforts ended, the Yankees had gained nothing except heavy casualties and embarrassment. The only success they could claim was the burning of Legareville, a small undefended village of two dozen houses and two churches on Johns Island. This was the last major effort to capture Charleston, and South Carolina remained secure for several more months.

September 1864 saw the implementation of perhaps the cruelest and most despicable act by the U.S. Army when about six hundred captured Confederate officers were used as a human shield on the beach at Morris Island. These men, dubbed the "Immortal Six Hundred," suffered terribly at the hands of their captors until finally removed in October.

With Lincoln's reelection in November 1864, it was obvious the war would continue, and Sherman left Atlanta on his infamous "March to the Sea" campaign. Two substantial efforts to break the Charleston and Savannah Railroad in hopes of trapping Confederate forces in Savannah were foiled. At the Battle of Honey Hill on November 30, the Union advance was decisively stopped by an outnumbered ragtag Confederate force that inflicted about eight hundred casualties while incurring less than fifty of their own. A week later, another Union force received an embarrassing defeat in the Battle of Tulifinny Creek despite having a five-to-one advantage in numbers. Though Savannah fell to Sherman on December 21, the year ended with South Carolina's interior unsullied and Union forces still restricted to the coastal areas. Little had changed militarily in the previous three years.

The year 1865 began ominously with Sherman's troops hurling vile threats about what they intended to do in South Carolina. Just two weeks earlier, Sherman had written to U.S. Grant, "With Savannah in our possession… we can punish South Carolina as she deserves.…I do sincerely believe that the whole of the United States, North and South, would rejoice to have this army turned loose on South Carolina to devastate that state, in the same manner as have done in Georgia."[1]

The end of January 1865 marked the beginning of what is known as the Carolinas Campaign, with Sherman's army leaving Savannah and Union troops from Beaufort advancing into the interior regions previously denied them. Their first actions were to loot and burn farms and settlements. Grahamville, Robertsville, Gillisonville, Lawtonville and McPhersonville were destroyed. A small Confederate force fought a delaying action at Rivers Bridge on February 3, the only substantial attempt made in the state against Sherman's march. The last major action took place in Aiken on February 11, when Confederates secured victory in a cavalry action. From that point on, there was no organized resistance to the Union advance. Farther inland, Barnwell, Blackville and Orangeburg were set afire after pillaging by the Yankee juggernaut. On February 17, Confederate forces evacuated Charleston. That same day, Columbia was captured by Sherman's troops, and that night the city was pillaged and burned. Sherman and his senior commanders did little to prevent atrocities and depredations of every kind as the army continued its march toward North Carolina. Winnsboro was looted and burned. Civilians, Black and White alike, in towns, villages or remote farms were subjected to every form of abuse, including murder, by Sherman's unrestrained troops. Cheraw, Chesterfield, Florence, Society Hill, Darlington and other areas suffered horribly before the Yankee hordes crossed over into North Carolina in early March, leaving behind a swath of destruction over forty miles wide.

On April 5, a Union force from recently occupied Georgetown set forth to raid the state's already damaged interior. Potter's Raid, named for its commanding officer General Edward E. Potter of New York, was tasked primarily with destroying food supplies and railway capability but went well beyond that during the raid. The Yankees roamed at will, terrorizing the civilian population while looting and pillaging at every opportunity. Farms, crops, livestock, mills, warehouses, railway equipment and over fifty thousand bales of cotton were destroyed all along the path extending to Camden before it ended three weeks after commencement.

Yet there was another raid by Union cavalry. Major General George Stoneman, another New Yorker and Stonewall Jackson's roommate at West Point but a dismal failure in combat operations throughout the war, was sent forth in late March from Knoxville under orders to "destroy, not fight" and to "dismantle the country." Stoneman and his force of six thousand cavalrymen terrorized the citizens in the mountains of east Tennessee, much of North Carolina and southwestern Virginia. The surrender of Confederate armies in April under Generals Robert E. Lee and Joseph Johnston did not deter him or his work. In early May, after wreaking havoc in those states by burning, pillaging, murdering and causing destruction everywhere they went, Stoneman's men entered the upcountry of South Carolina. There, they continued their villainy at Spartanburg, Greenville and Anderson before finally returning to Knoxville.

The wanton devastation by Union forces across South Carolina in just four months of 1865 left a lasting mark for decades. All this was soon followed up by Union occupation across the state. With the collapse of the Confederacy, South Carolina's citizens found themselves ruled not by law but by the bayonet of the Union occupiers. In early 1867, even this this was not enough for the Radicals in Washington, D.C., and in March that year, an even tighter grip was set in place with the advent of Reconstruction, an ordeal filled with grief, torment and anguish lasting until 1877. The state did not fully recover from the horrors of war, occupation and Reconstruction until the mid-twentieth century.

Not everyone in South Carolina "went off to war," but those who remained at home certainly became involved in it. When the man of a family marched away, his wife and children had to step up and perform the tasks he normally filled. Boys were soon doing the plowing, wives began handling the planning and financial matters and girls took charge of other household responsibilities. Most plantations and farms planted sustenance crops in lieu of cash crops such as cotton.

The war effort in support of the troops was immense and showed solidarity in every way. Women and girls of every age across the state coordinated their efforts in gathering material for weaving and manufacturing shirts, socks and other items of apparel for the troops. When shortages of medicines hit, they planted medicinal gardens and searched the woods for medicinal plants. Fairs were conducted to raise money for what was needed to support the men in gray. The Ladies Association in Charleston raised so much money to support the building of the gunboat *Charleston* that it was nicknamed the "Ladies Gunboat." Support from the Ladies Associations across the state was vitally important. From large cities like Charleston and Columbia to small towns like Eutawville and Fairfield, they provided much of what the Confederate government could not.

Wayside hospitals, located at railroad depots, were critically acclaimed. Nearly all were formed by ladies' groups to provide basic needs for soldiers in transit, including meals and medical care for sick or wounded. Larger depots often had overnight accommodations and medical staffs. These wayside hospitals benefited greatly from the donations of food, clothing, bandages, medicine and nursing assistance from the ladies. The Columbia Wayside Hospital was the largest in the state and served an estimated seventy-five thousand men during the war. It made no difference which state the soldier came from, the ladies were there for him. Sarah Rowe of Orangeburg made the care of soldiers her personal mission during the war and earned the nickname the "Soldier's Friend." Mary Snowden of Charleston was just as dedicated and earned similar respect, but there were literally thousands of others who gave freely and worked tirelessly in support of these projects.

Some men did not join the military. Many were too old, others too young. A small number, like ironworkers, educators, physicians, railroad workers and others in specified professions, were exempt from service. Still, they usually formed the local militia or home guard, and late in the war, some found themselves in action against Union troops and performed valiantly, especially during Potter's Raid.

Civilian life in South Carolina's interior became more spartan as the war progressed and hardships arose. Relief societies, some state-run and others run by the ladies, tried to provide for families in dire need or otherwise destitute. Still, life across most of the state went on as usual. County courts, state and local governments and public affairs such as elections carried on without interruption until early 1865, when Union troops finally reached the state's interior, bringing havoc and ruin with them.

Areas affected by the wanton destruction from Sherman's march and the follow-up Union raids suffered greatly. Homes, mills, factories and farms were burned; livestock was taken or slaughtered; storehouses of food were stolen or destroyed; and the citizens affected were left with only the clothing they wore as the Union army departed. Untold thousands of civilians of both races, homeless with no provisions in the midst of winter, endured horrendous hardships and uncertain futures. Their woes were just beginning, as shortly afterward came Union occupation and Reconstruction, both of which brought more gloom and despair.

2

THE EARLY DAYS

THE FIRST CASUALTY

South Carolina seceded from the Union on December 20, 1860. This action led U.S. Army major Robert Anderson, commander of the small contingent in Charleston headquartered at Fort Moultrie on Sullivan's Island, to abandon Fort Moultrie and move his garrison to Fort Sumter. The surreptitious method in which he performed this move, without orders or consultation with his superiors in Washington, D.C., had tremendous repercussions.

Anderson moved his men secretly on the night of December 26. Before leaving Fort Moultrie, he ordered that the forts' guns be spiked, the carriages for those guns facing Fort Sumter be burned and the flagpole within the fort be cut down. The next day, Governor Francis Pickens, disturbed by these unwarranted and devious acts, ordered his militia to take control of Fort Moultrie as well as long-abandoned Fort Johnson and Castle Pinckney, each a key position in Charleston's harbor. On December 30, the U.S. Arsenal in downtown Charleston was seized. Tensions and anxiety in Charleston were high, and the militia was on full alert.

The Charleston Light Infantry was one of the militia commands that took control of Castle Pinckney and then garrisoned it. Among its numbers was Private Robert Little Holmes, a lifelong Charlestonian and successful businessman. Holmes, at age thirty, was in his prime with a promising future.

FORT SUMPTER, CHARLESTON HARBOR, IN POSSESSION OF

ERSON A SKETCH TAKEN FROM FORT MOULTRIE, BY OUR SPECIAL ARTIST NOW IN CHARLESTON.—SEE PAGE 151.

Castle Pinckney in Charleston's harbor. *Library of Congress.*

Unfortunately, that future ended suddenly and tragically with his death at Castle Pinckney on January 7, 1861. The *Charleston Mercury* reported the story two days later, captioned by a headline intended to capture attention.

> *Terrible Accident at Castle Pinckney—First Casualty of the War*
> *We are pained to record, that on Monday night, shortly after 10 o'clock, as one of the sentinels at Castle Pinckney was going on his rounds, he was approached by a person then unknown. The sentinel presented his musket in the act of challenging him, when the piece unfortunately went off, and the stranger immediately fell. On examination, it proved to be Private R.L. Holmes, of the Carolina Light Infantry. The ball had taken effect in the left side under the shoulder, traversing both lungs, and inflicting a wound from the effects of which he survived only twenty minutes.*

The same day the article on Holmes's death appeared, the Union supply ship *Star of the West* was fired on as it attempted to enter Charleston's harbor with supplies and reinforcements for Major Anderson and his garrison at Fort Sumter. Private Holmes, one of five brothers who wore the gray, was buried in Charleston's Magnolia Cemetery. Three of his brothers survived the war, but another was killed in action at Gaines Mill in 1862.

The Schooner *Rhoda H. Shannon* Incident

Historians have written a great deal about the guns of Morris Island firing at the U.S. supply vessel *Star of the West* on January 9, 1861, and then again on Fort Sumter the following April 12. However, in between those events, those same guns were involved in another action, one seldom mentioned but quite concerning at the time.

It began when the 180-ton schooner *Rhoda H. Shannon* left Boston on March 26 bound for Savannah with a shipment of ice. Bad weather during the voyage prevented navigational fixes and the ship's master, Joseph Marts, on seeing Charleston's harbor on the afternoon of April 3, mistook the harbor entrance as Tybee Island at the mouth of the Savannah River. His arrival in the "midst of a gale that had been blowing for several days" was another piece of bad luck, as the waters were said to be "white with foam." Sighting a pilot boat, he sent a man to the bow to wave the U.S. flag as a request for a pilot to come aboard. When one didn't arrive, the master made a poor decision by deciding to enter the port on his own, thus setting off a series of events he soon came to regret.

As the schooner neared Morris Island, guns from the Confederate emplacements there fired several shots across his bow. Realizing his ship was not flying its colors and thinking that was the cause for the firing, he hastily raised the U.S. flag. To his great surprise, the guns began firing at the ship, scoring several near-misses. The befuddled master turned his ship and beat a retreat before anchoring just inside the Charleston bar and trying to discover what was going on.

Major Robert Anderson, commanding U.S. forces in Fort Sumter, sent the fort's boat with an officer to Morris Island to obtain an explanation for the firing and to request permission to visit the schooner. Lieutenant Colonel W.G. DeSaussure, commanding Confederate forces on Morris Island, advised that he was under orders to prevent any ship flying the U.S. flag from entering the harbor. DeSaussure sent a revenue cutter to ascertain damage to the *Shannon*, and Anderson's boat followed. The master explained his actions and admitted confusion. Both sides accepted his story and were relieved no harm or casualties were incurred in light of the facts. DeSaussure gave assurances the vessel "would not be molested" if it sought safety from the weather and anchored in the harbor, but the *Shannon* soon headed to sea and disappeared from sight.

Confederate authorities explained the situation quickly to Charleston's citizens to ease their anxieties and stop rumors that the schooner was attempting a resupply of Fort Sumter in advance of a fleet of U.S. warships. It was all just a case of bad weather, bad luck and bad judgment.[2]

U.S. OFFICERS AT FORT SUMTER IN APRIL 1861

Much has been written on Major Robert Anderson, the U.S. commander at Fort Sumter during the bombardment by Confederate forces. A study of the eight officers under his command and present during the bombardment finds some interesting details. Anderson and six others were West Point graduates. All eight subordinate officers served Anderson well before and during the bombardment. Of special interest is seeing how each man fared as the war progressed.

Major Anderson was quickly promoted to brigadier general and ultimately breveted as a major general, though he never again led troops

U.S. officers at Fort Sumter, April 12, 1861. *Library of Congress.*

or faced battle as a general. Captain John Foster, better known for his infamous "Immortal Six Hundred" implementation in 1864, ended the war as a breveted major general, as did Captain Abner Doubleday. Captain Truman Seymour was breveted brigadier general and later commanded the assault on Battery Wagner for which he received a wound and much criticism.

First Lieutenant Jefferson C. Davis (no relation to the president of the Confederacy) was the only officer at the fort without a college degree. His commission resulted from bravery as a sergeant in the Mexican-American War. Breveted major general, he was fortunate to have been in the army at all after murdering a commanding officer in 1862 and somehow escaping the consequences. Second Lieutenant Norman J. Hall, appointed to West Point in 1854 by Secretary of War Jefferson F. Davis (future president of the Confederacy), rose to the rank of colonel. He likely would have become a general, but his health deteriorated to such an extent that he left the army in late 1863 and died in 1865. The fort's surgeon, Samuel W. Crawford, with a medical degree from the University of Pennsylvania and in army service since 1851, left the medical profession for the infantry and was ultimately breveted as a major general.

Two promising young officers died within a year of Fort Sumter's surrender. Lieutenant George W. Snyder was breveted captain but died of disease in November 1861. Lieutenant Theodore Talbot became a major, serving as an assistant adjutant general before dying of tuberculosis in April 1862.

The ninth officer at Sumter was Second Lieutenant Richard K. Meade, an engineer whose story is much different than the others. Meade received notable praise for his courage and ingenuity during Sumter's bombardment. However, he was a Virginian, and when Virginia seceded, Meade resigned from the U.S. Army and immediately offered his services to his beloved state. Initially appointed first lieutenant of artillery, he soon was transferred to the Engineer Department, where he received promotions to captain in February 1862 and to major the following June. Unfortunately, his high-quality service was cut short by typhoid fever, which caused his death in July 1862. Meade was one of four West Point graduates to fight for both the Union and the Confederacy.[3]

SURRENDER OF FORT SUMTER: THE REST OF THE STORY

History books have long recorded the firing on Fort Sumter by Confederate forces on April 12, 1861, and its surrender the next day. They usually mention surrender terms allowed the U.S. garrison to conduct a one-hundred-gun salute before lowering the U.S. garrison flag and departing the fort on April 14. Some go further by noting the salute became terribly marred when a man was killed by premature explosion of a cannon. But there is even more to this story.

The explosion occurred on the forty-third shot (some sources state the forty-seventh) of the salute when a powder charge rammed into a cannon was ignited by sparks that apparently blew into the barrel from fires at the fort. The resulting explosion ignited cartridges nearby, resulting in another fire and explosions sending men tumbling through the air. This tragic accident led to the salute being halted at fifty shots, as the carnage dampened the mood of the event. Private Daniel Hough was killed almost instantly, and five others sustained injuries. Private Edward Galloway was taken to a Charleston hospital with severe wounds and died a week later. Private James Fielding was also hospitalized with wounds and burns. He eventually recovered from his injuries and was "sent north without exchange." The other three injured men were able to depart the fort with the garrison.[4]

Private Hough is said to have been buried on Fort Sumter's parade ground by the U.S. garrison before it departed the fort. Why his body was not carried away when the garrison departed is not explained. However, numerous efforts by his family to locate and recover his remains have been fruitless. There is speculation he was later removed by the Confederates to a cemetery on Sullivan's Island or perhaps the St. Lawrence Cemetery in Charleston. Some think his grave remained at Fort Sumter but was "lost" in the 1863–64 Union bombardments of the fort. Unfortunately, his final resting site remains a mystery. Hough, an Irish immigrant who arrived in New York in 1849 and immediately enlisted in the army, is generally recognized as the first U.S. casualty of the war.

The whereabouts of Private Galloway's remains are also unknown despite numerous efforts to find his grave. No record regarding his burial site has been located. Historians consider Galloway the first man to be mortally wounded in the war.

CAPTAIN DUNCAN N. INGRAHAM, CSN

A Man to Be Remembered

The U.S. Navy has long honored notable Americans by naming warships after them. Leading the list is George Washington with eight ships bearing his name. Stephen Decatur has five. Close behind is a small group of others with four ships named for them. Included on this short list are three former presidents (Thomas Jefferson, James Madison and U.S. Grant) and Duncan N. Ingraham, a native Charlestonian and former Confederate commodore.

Ingraham, born in 1802, came from a seafaring family. His father, a close friend of John Paul Jones, moved his family from Massachusetts to Charleston after the

Captain Duncan N. Ingraham, CSN. *Library of Congress.*

Revolutionary War. Ingraham married the granddaughter of Henry Laurens, a South Carolina Patriot and president of the Continental Congress. He fathered eleven children, three of whom served the Confederacy. Ingraham began his naval career in 1812 as a nine-year-old midshipman and, over time, rose in the ranks to captain in the U.S. Navy with command of a warship. In 1853, his name became internationally known when he rescued a Hungarian wanting to obtain U.S. citizenship being held captive on an Austrian warship at the port of Smyrna, Turkey. In a tense and stunning diplomatic action, his stance in this well-documented incident known as the Koszta Affair became a precedent in international law. For this, he received special thanks in form of a Congressional Gold Medal and similar tributes from other organizations and groups. In 1856, he served as chief of the Bureau of Ordnance and Hydrography for the navy.

In January 1861, South Carolina took steps to establish a Coast Police to protect its coast and inlets. Some records call the organization the South Carolina Navy. Captain Ingraham, who submitted his resignation from the U.S. Navy shortly after South Carolina seceded from the union, was chosen to make this force a reality.

Building the South Carolina Navy from ground up was no easy task, but by the late spring of 1861, Ingraham had secured the services of seasoned officers, midshipmen, surgeons and engineers. He obtained and outfitted six vessels manned by full crews, which were turned over to the Confederate navy when the South Carolina Navy was dis-established. Ingraham was then placed in command of Charleston's Naval Station. In January 1863, with his flag on the ironclad CSS *Palmetto State* and supported by the CSS *Chicora*, he led a successful attack on the Union blockading ships off Charleston's coast. All in all, his leadership and organizational skills were invaluable to the defense of Charleston and the progress of the C.S. Navy. After the war, Ingraham remained in Charleston and, on his death, was buried in the city's venerable Magnolia Cemetery.

Despite his Confederate service, his fame and reputation lived on and was formally acknowledged by the U.S. Navy in the early twentieth century with the first USS *Ingraham* (DD-111), a destroyer. Built for World War I, it was commissioned shortly after the war's end. Like many ships from that war, it was soon placed in reserve and eventually sold for scrap in 1936. The second *Ingraham* (DD-444), also a destroyer, was commissioned and sponsored by Ingraham's granddaughter in 1941. The ship provided World War II service in the Atlantic until a tragic

USS *Ingraham* (DD-694). *Naval History & Heritage Command.*

collision caused it to sink with great loss of life in 1944. The third *Ingraham* (DD-694), another destroyer, was commissioned in 1944 and again sponsored by Ingraham's granddaughter. This vessel sailed the seas in stellar fashion with substantial wartime action in World War II, Korea and Vietnam before being retired in 1971. The final *Ingraham* (FFG-61), a guided missile frigate, saw solid and commendable active service spanning 1989 to 2015.[5]

SHIPS OF SOUTH CAROLINA'S NAVY

Quickly following secession, South Carolina formed a command called the Coast Police. Starting from scratch, it soon had six vessels fully manned by seasoned officers and crewmen. The vessels remained in state service until

May 1861, when they were turned over to the Confederacy. Little attention has been afforded the ships involved, but three of them provided service worthy of mention.

The flotilla included, among others, the *Lady Davis*, the *General Clinch* and the *Gordon*. By early April 1861, each was lightly armed and commanded by a Confederate naval officer though the vessels and crews were in the state's Coast Police. On April 5, 1861, a week before Confederate forces fired on Fort Sumter and with knowledge of a possible Union relief force destined for Charleston, they received orders to prepare for sea and take on board "as much fuel as possible and ten day's provisions." Additional orders called for them to take station off Charleston's main shipping channel "to guard the approaches to this harbor from the sea and prevent a reinforcement of Fort Sumter." Each morning at daylight, they were to get underway, go as far as Bull's Bay and stay offshore ten to fifteen miles watching for threats. At night, they were to anchor off Sullivan's Island and remain alert for any nighttime attempt by U.S. ships to slip into the harbor. While their mission was primarily to provide early warning, they were fully authorized to fire their guns, "making them tell upon the enemy" if the situation required it.[6]

Two warships and a transport of the Union relief force arrived off Charleston in the early morning of April 12, several hours after the firing on Fort Sumter began. They could only watch the engagement and await arrival of the other vessels of the expedition. Two other warships and a tug eventually arrived in the next couple of days. One wonders what would have happened had any or all of the expedition's ships arrived a day or two earlier in the daytime. Would the first shots of the war have been a few miles off Charleston's harbor?

After Fort Sumter was captured, two of the Confederate vessels were officially transferred to the C.S. Navy. The *Lady Davis* provided excellent service around Beaufort in 1861 before returning to Charleston. The engines were given to the ironclad CSS *Palmetto State* in late 1862, and *Lady Davis* was sold to private interests. Refitted as a blockade runner, it proved a success in this new role. The versatile *General Clinch* was used by the C.S. Navy as a tender, harbor transport and patrol boat. It was repurposed as a blockade runner in late 1864 and sailed from Charleston to Nassau, where it remained until the war ended.

The third vessel was the fine steamer *Gordon*, originally a trader serving Charleston and Wilmington, which was quickly converted to a privateer. It was mentioned frequently in both Northern and Southern newspapers during the summer of 1861 for its work in that role. Armed with three heavy guns, *Gordon* took five U.S. flagged merchant vessels as war prizes. Purchased by the Confederacy in early 1862 and renamed the *Theodora*, this steamer sailed as a government-owned blockade runner until captured off Wilmington in May 1862.

LIEUTENANT ALEXANDER R. CHISOLM

Beauregard's Aide-de-Camp Extraordinaire

Each Confederate brigade, division or corps had an assigned staff formed by appointments from the various offices in the War Department. Generals commanding these units had little say as to who served on the staff since it belonged to the unit he commanded, not to him. The lone exception was the aide-de-camp (ADC), who was appointed by and served at the pleasure of the general. An ADC received the rank of first lieutenant and served as the most junior officer on staff, all the while knowing there were no provisions for promotion. His duties were simply whatever the general assigned him. If the general died, resigned or lost his command, the ADC was immediately off staff and subject to conscription unless another position could be quickly found.

Generals invariably selected a relative or close friend, someone they had full trust in, as their ADC. South Carolina's generals followed this pattern. Matthew C. Butler and Wade Hampton appointed their brothers. Micah Jenkins selected a brother-in-law. Stephen Elliott selected a close friend who had also served as a sergeant for over two years in his artillery battery.

General P.G.T. Beauregard broke from this pattern by appointing a South Carolinian, Beaufort native Alexander R. Chisolm, as his ADC. The men first met only in February 1861 at Charleston when Chisolm, a civilian, was selected by Governor Pickens to assist in the erection of emplacements at Cummings Point on Morris Island. Beauregard was so impressed with Chisolm that he appointed him as his ADC a month later, thus forging a friendship and professional relationship unmatched anywhere in the army.

Chisolm was present when Fort Sumter was captured in April 1861. Beauregard's full trust in him from the earliest days is demonstrated by Chisolm's selection as one of the three officers sent to Sumter by Beauregard asking for its surrender before it was fired on. Educated and articulate, he often served as Beauregard's personal emissary and efficiently handled assignments normally reserved for officers of higher rank when necessary. Trustworthy, diligent and competent in all he was assigned, Chisolm became Beauregard's "confidential friend" as well as a valued staff member. Beauregard, as a ranking general, was allowed additional ADCs as the war continued, but Chisolm remained his primary ADC and close confidant.

Chisolm followed Beauregard to his various posts. At First Manassas, Chisolm, while acting as a courier, found himself deeply involved with the battle. At one point, he rallied panicked soldiers and got them reorganized as an effective command. He also, without orders, served as a battlefield guide for arriving forces that day. He was at Shiloh, the siege of Charleston, Petersburg and the Carolinas Campaign. In early 1865, Beauregard asked the War Department to promote Chisolm to major, a request that was unprecedented for an ADC. President Jefferson Davis gave a positive endorsement, but the war ended before a promotion could be placed into effect.

Most staff officers served with a particular general just a year or two. Chisolm served as Beauregard's ADC from March 12, 1861, to his parole at Greensboro on May 1, 1865, a period of nearly fifty consecutive months. This South Carolinian was the most senior lieutenant and ADC in the entire army. No other staff officer in the army had such tenure.[7]

CONFEDERATE GUNBOAT ON THE ATTACK

In May 1861, the Confederate navy was in its infancy but had bold and seasoned leadership. One of its few assets was a small iron-hulled vessel built for use as a steam tug in 1858 named the *James Gray*. Purchased by the State of South Carolina in March 1861 and renamed *Lady Davis*, the 250-ton vessel was armed with a twenty-four-pounder cannon and a twelve-pounder rifled gun. It was transferred to the Confederacy on May 7, 1861, under command of Lieutenant Thomas P. Pelot (pronounced Pee-low). A native Charlestonian and an 1857 graduate of the U.S. Naval Academy, Pelot resigned his commission in the U.S. Navy in January 1861 and quickly accepted a commission in the C.S. Navy.

On May 19, just twelve days after taking command, Lieutenant Pelot displayed his mettle by taking his little vessel from Beaufort in search of the armed brig USS *Perry*, a U.S. warship said to be lurking off the coast of Port Royal Sound. Before sailing, he took aboard Captain (later Brigadier General) Stephen Elliott as his pilot and a detachment of Elliott's Beaufort Volunteer Artillery armed with muskets to serve as marines for the expected engagement. The *Perry* was not found, but the U.S.-flagged merchant ship *A.B. Thompson* was intercepted, boarded and taken as a war prize back to Beaufort.

This one-day expedition was the first high seas offensive action of the war by the Confederate navy. The *A.B. Thompson* was the first war prize taken by either side. While the action was hailed by the South, Northern politicians and press were enraged, calling the seizure an act of piracy while describing the *Lady Davis* as a privateer. Crewmen of the unfortunate merchantman were held by the Confederate government through the summer until being exchanged for Southern civilians held captive by U.S. authorities.[8]

Lieutenant Pelot and Captain Elliott each achieved additional acclaim later in their service. Pelot planned and led the attack in which the USS *Water Witch* was boarded and captured near Savannah. Unfortunately, he was killed in this action and buried in Savannah. Pelot is honored in a memorial to South Carolina Naval Heroes in Charleston's Magnolia Cemetery. Captain Elliott rose to fame for his defense of Fort Sumter from September 1863 to May 1864, and shortly afterward, he was appointed brigadier general.

3

LEADERSHIP

Seven Generals from the Hampton Legion

South Carolina's Hampton Legion was a premier unit of the Confederate army. Formed and personally outfitted by Wade Hampton, it consisted of a battalion of infantry, another of cavalry and a two-gun section of artillery. Though it never fought as a single unit, its men and officers provided splendid service throughout the war. Further, the Confederacy appointed seven generals from its ranks, more than from any other single unit. All but one were native South Carolinians. A brief synopsis shows how much leadership talent was in the Legion.

WADE HAMPTON STARTED THE war as colonel of the legion and distinguished himself in every way possible throughout the war. Promoted to brigadier general of infantry in May 1862, he was transferred at that rank to the cavalry a few months later. In August 1863, Hampton was promoted to major general and, following the death of JEB Stuart, commanded the

Lieutenant General Wade Hampton III. *Library of Congress.*

cavalry corps of the Army of Northern Virginia in a splendid manner. Upon transfer to South Carolina in February 1865 to face Sherman's advance, Hampton was promoted to lieutenant general. Despite having no military experience of any sort before the war, Hampton emerged as one of the finest officers of the Confederacy.

STEPHEN DILL LEE, an 1850 graduate of West Point, had service with the Hampton Legion only briefly because General P.G.T Beauregard, who knew and favored him, offered him command of an artillery battery in Virginia. Lee went on to serve in infantry and cavalry commands, making him a highly versatile officer. Promoted to brigadier general in 1862, major general in 1863 and lieutenant general in early 1865, he served in both the eastern and western theaters of war with much acclaim.

MATTHEW C. BUTLER was promoted to captain in the Legion Cavalry in early 1862 and, when it was blended into the new Second South Carolina Cavalry Regiment, he was appointed as its colonel. Promoted to brigadier general in early 1864, he rose to major general later that same year. Butler distinguished himself as a solid officer at all levels of command.

MARTIN W. GARY began his service as a captain in the Legion Infantry battalion and in 1862 rose to lieutenant colonel in command followed by promotion to colonel when the battalion was increased to a full regiment. In 1864, the Hampton Legion Infantry was redesignated the Hampton Legion Cavalry, and Gary was promoted to brigadier general. Gary's wartime service was one showing much personal courage and strong leadership.

JAMES JOHNSTON PETTIGREW, a North Carolina native, lived in Charleston from 1856 until the war began. Enlisting in the legion, he served as a private prior to answering an offer to take command of the Twenty-Second North Carolina Infantry in August 1861. Promoted to brigadier general in 1862, he served with distinction and courage. At Gettysburg, he led Heth's Division in Pickett's Charge. Pettigrew died of wounds received during the withdrawal from Gettysburg to Virginia.

THOMAS M. LOGAN rose from private to captain in the Hampton Legion Infantry in 1861. He was noted for superb leadership in many battles throughout the war. At Sharpsburg, he was cited for "great bravery." Promotions to major and lieutenant colonel followed quickly in late 1862. He received promotion to colonel in May 1864 and brigadier general at age twenty-four in early 1865.

JAMES CONNER served as a captain and major in the Legion Infantry Battalion, and he was appointed colonel of the Twenty-Second North Carolina Infantry regiment in 1862. He distinguished himself at

Chancellorsville and Gettysburg and was promoted to brigadier general in June 1864. His service, too-often overlooked, is most admirable.

THREE CONFEDERATE GENERALS WITH THE RIGHT STUFF

Just eighty-three brigadier generals in the entire Confederate army were promoted to the rank of major general during the War for Southern Independence. These promotions were based on meritorious leadership and personal bravery. Most possessed two other personal qualifications: (1) established battle or campaign experience from the Indian wars or the Mexican-American War as officers and (2) a college education. It should be no surprise that fifty-seven of them were graduates of the U.S. Military Academy at West Point. A close review of the remainder finds twenty-three having at least one of these qualifications, and quite a few had both. Clearly the army sought educated men with meaningful military exposure to fill its higher levels of leadership. However, three others were promoted despite having spent neither a day in college nor possessing a substantial prewar military background. Two are well-known, but the third might very well be a surprise.

The first name on this short list is the incomparable Nathan Bedford Forrest of Tennessee. Forrest lost his father at age sixteen and became the man of his house, caring and providing for his siblings and mother. Enlisting as a private in 1861, he rose to lieutenant colonel and then progressively to lieutenant general. Forrest's exploits are legendary and well-chronicled. He is known as the "Wizard of the Saddle," and most historians consider him the best cavalry officer of the war in either army.

The next man is Patrick Cleburne, who earned the nickname "Stonewall of the West" for his superb service as an infantry brigade and division commander. Cleburne, an Irish immigrant who was orphaned at age fifteen, served three years in the English army as an enlisted man but never left Ireland, and most of his enlistment was as a prison guard. He immigrated to the United States in 1850 and settled in Arkansas. Cleburne became a colonel in the Confederate army in 1861, a brigadier general in 1862 and a major general in 1863. General Robert E. Lee likened his service and rapid promotion as "a meteor shining from a clouded sky." Cleburne provided distinguished service in nearly every major battle of the Army of Tennessee until his death in the November 1864 Battle of Franklin, Tennessee.

Concluding this small group is South Carolinian Joseph Brevard Kershaw of Camden. Kershaw never attended college but possessed sufficient education and personal attributes to became a lawyer at age twenty-one. His military service as a lieutenant in the Palmetto Regiment during the Mexican-American War was quickly cut short by disease, which led to his early return home without any significant military experience.

Kershaw was elected colonel of the Second South Carolina Infantry in 1861, promoted to brigadier general in February 1862 and then raised to major general June 1864. He saw action in nearly all the battles of the Army of Northern Virginia. Prominent historians since the war's end have rated him as one of the very best brigade and division commanders of the Confederacy. One wrote that "[Kershaw] repeatedly demonstrated he was without peer as a combat leader."[9]

These three men, altogether different in temperament and personality, were chosen as major generals after close scrutiny from the highest levels for their exceptional leadership. Their later service fully justified their selection.

MAJOR GENERAL MATTHEW C. BUTLER

Next to the incomparable Wade Hampton III, Matthew Calbraith Butler was South Carolina's most prominent cavalry commander in the War for Southern Independence. Described as a "Gentleman, Statesman and Soldier," Butler was connected to several generations of distinguished families through each of his parents. Growing up in Edgefield, South Carolina, he was depicted as quite handsome and a superb orator. He graduated from South Carolina College and was admitted to the state bar in 1857.

Butler joined the Hampton Legion Cavalry Battalion and was elected captain of his company in June 1861. A month later, he received promotion to major. The battalion was active in Virginia in 1861 with scouting, picketing duties and occasional skirmishes, but the summer of 1862 saw it in action at Second Manassas and in the Maryland Campaign. In October of that year, the cavalry arm of the Army of Northern Virginia was increased from a brigade to a division. In this reorganization, the Hampton Legion Cavalry lost its identity when it merged with another command to form the Second South Carolina Cavalry, and Butler was selected as its colonel.

Butler performed well in General J.E.B. Stuart's famous raids on Chambersburg and Dumfries in late 1862 and saw action at Fredericksburg

Major General Matthew C. Butler.
Library of Congress.

that year. His skillful leadership and personal courage in the Battle of Brandy Station (June 9, 1863) showed his merits as a battlefield leader in full for the first time. Unfortunately, a cannon shell took off his right foot in that battle, leading to a lengthy rehabilitation period.

Despite this injury, his past service warranted serious consideration for promotion to brigadier general. Hampton's succinct recommendation for Butler's promotion simply covered all aspects of Butler's qualifications: "I have not seen a better officer in the [cavalry] service." Hampton did not take great pains pointing out Butler's personal courage, his ability to lead men or his battlefield skills, as they were apparently known to all. Stuart's endorsement was remarkably similar and said, "Colonel Butler has always been distinguished for gallantry....I know of no one better able or worthy." The promotion was authorized on September 1, 1863, while Butler was home recovering.[10]

Butler returned to Virginia in early May 1864 at the head of a brand-new, full-strength, largely untested cavalry brigade consisting of the Fourth, Fifth and Sixth South Carolina Cavalry regiments. The brigade found itself in battle almost from point of arrival. Armed with three-band rifled muskets used by infantry, the men fought mostly dismounted in numerous and intense engagements. During the summer of 1864, Butler's Brigade was involved in victories against a variety of top Union cavalry commanders, including Sheridan, Wilson and Gregg. The brigade especially distinguished itself at Trevilian Station (June 11–12), the largest all-cavalry battle in the war, and again at Ream's Station (August 25). It also performed well in a host of lesser engagements, earning great praise and recognition.

General Hampton, upon being named to command the cavalry corps of the Army of Northern Virginia in August 1864, urged promotion of Butler to succeed him in command of his former division. Butler's long record of personal courage, battlefield leadership and the respect given him by all ranks within his brigade warranted such an appointment to major general.

Robert E. Lee's endorsement of the nomination dated September 28, 1864, reads in part, "[Butler] has shown great gallantry and manages his troops with skill."[11] The War Department confirmed the appointment and issued the well-deserved promotion the following December.

That same month, a massive Union force began moving southward from Petersburg toward Hicksford (now Emporia), Virginia, with plans to break the Weldon Railroad. In a campaign known widely as the "Applejack Raid," the Yankees marched through Sussex County, farmland previously untouched by war and blessed with a bountiful autumn harvest. They despoiled it by getting drunk, raping, murdering, looting and burning houses as they passed through. After having been foiled by Hampton and a small Confederate force at Hicksford, the Yankees repeated these despicable acts with even more fervor in their return to Petersburg.

Butler's scouts advised him of these outrages during the initial advance and asked for guidance. There was nothing in the army's manuals about dealing with such situations. Butler certainly knew of similar Union atrocities elsewhere across the South and was probably stressed that there was no sizeable Confederate force close enough to force an end to these depredations. Still, his response was reasoned and calculated as he became the first Southern general to issue an order that can best be termed "righteous retribution."

Butler's response to the scouts was likely the most profound and reluctant order he ever issued. It called for any Yankees caught in the act of these atrocities, whether drunk or sober, to be swung by their arms and legs into the very flames they had started. Clear, simple and never rescinded, this order was used by his scouts liberally over the next few days and again against Sherman's "bummers" in the Carolinas Campaign in 1865. There were no postwar repercussions by the United States against Butler for taking this measure.[12]

Butler showed he was as an efficient and capable commander of a division as he was of a brigade and continued to justify the unwavering trust of Hampton from the time of his promotion through the Carolinas Campaign and the end of the war. Paroled on May 1, 1865, at Greensboro following Johnston's surrender to Sherman, Butler returned home to resume his law practice. Politically active before, during and after Reconstruction, he served three terms as U.S. senator, earning respect from all quarters. In 1898, Butler was called into military service again but this time as a major general in the U.S. Army during the Spanish-American War. His later years saw him resume his law practice.

Matthew C. Butler left behind a legacy of service to South Carolina in both war and peace. He was eminently qualified and successful in the three major phases of his life's work. Excelling as an attorney, as a soldier and as a member of the U.S. Senate, he is deserving of our remembrance.

MAJOR GENERAL JOSEPH B. KERSHAW

General Kershaw emerged from the War Between the States with the reputation of being one of the premier generals in the Army of Northern Virginia. Detailed studies by numerous postwar scholars and historians ever since have reached the same conclusion. Ed Bearss, one of the nation's most prominent historians of the war, wrote, "Few if any units were more capable or terrible in battle as Kershaw's Brigade." He added, "[Kershaw] repeatedly demonstrated he was without peer as a combat leader."[13]

A native of Camden, South Carolina, and the grandson of the Revolutionary War hero for whom Kershaw County was named, General Kershaw lost his father at age seven. Making the best of his secondary school education, he passed the bar exam in 1843 without attending college. Hard work, a keen and clear-thinking mind along with a gentlemanly and approachable countenance were among his lifelong attributes. He was described as a man of high character, morally worthy, zealous and true. Kershaw served briefly in the Mexican-American War as a lieutenant in South Carolina's famed Palmetto Regiment. Politically active, he served in the state legislature and as a member of the 1860 Secession Convention. Additionally, his militia unit elected him as its colonel in 1859, and on forming the Second South Carolina Volunteers in early 1861, he was elected colonel of the regiment.

He and his regiment, at Charleston when Fort Sumter was taken in April 1861, were shortly afterward sent to Virginia. There they played a pivotal role in the First Battle of Manassas, bringing him much acclaim from, among others, Generals Jubal Early and James Longstreet. After his appointment as a brigadier general in February 1862, he and his superb brigade solidified their reputations at Savage's Station. His division commander, Major General Lafayette McLaws, wrote, "I beg leave to call attention to the gallantry, cool, yet daring, courage and skill in the management of his gallant command exhibited by General Kershaw."[14]

He received additional acclaim for action at Sharpsburg. At Fredericksburg, Kershaw assumed command at Marye's Heights when General Thomas Cobb was mortally wounded. On the second day at Gettysburg, amid the intense fighting in the Peach Orchard, his brigade fought stubbornly in confused fighting against a numerically superior foe. Continually adjusting the brigade alignment to allow his flanks to meet threats and establishing offensive coordination with other brigades at critical times, Kershaw displayed adeptness and superb battlefield skill.

In September 1863, Kershaw's Brigade moved with Lieutenant General James Longstreet to Georgia and was quickly in action at Chickamauga. The battle ended as a huge Confederate victory, and Kershaw again played a major role. In early November, Longstreet launched his Tennessee campaign, which resulted in several engagements, battle against the winter elements and an unsuccessful attempt to take Knoxville before going into winter quarters. Kershaw performed well under the adverse circumstances in this period and received promotion to major general in early 1864 just prior to Longstreet's Corps' return to Virginia.

At The Wilderness, he displayed confidence and skill in his first trial as a division commander and played a major role in saving the Army of Northern Virginia when A.P. Hill's Corps was routed. Other personal attributes attesting to his superb soldierly qualities were brought into play. His quick thinking, extraordinary personal courage and exemplary leadership were truly on display on May 6, 1864, at The Wilderness in an incident that was near disastrous. Kershaw was with General James Longstreet and a small party riding in front of Confederate lines after driving the enemy in disarray from the field. In the approaching darkness of the day, a North Carolina regiment unfortunately mistook the party for Union cavalry and fired on them. South Carolina's fine young general Micah Jenkins was killed, as were two of Kershaw's staff, and Longstreet was badly wounded. Jenkins's Brigade, thinking the firing was from a Union force, immediately took appropriate steps to return the fire. Kershaw quickly realized it was friendly fire and reacted with a split-second decision, placing his own safety in further jeopardy in a determined effort to defuse the situation and bring order to the scene.

Longstreet wrote, "Jenkins's brigade with levelled guns were in the act of returning fire…but as Kershaw's clear voice called 'f-r-i-e-n-d-s!', the arms were recovered without a shot in return." Kershaw wrote, "The leading files of Jenkins' brigade…instantly faced the firing and were about to return it." He added, "I dashed my horse into their ranks crying, 'They are friends.'"

The North Carolinians, on seeing and hearing Kershaw and realizing what they had done, fired no more. Kershaw's prompt and crucial actions in those tense moments prevented an even deeper calamity. Riding in the open in such a confused and volatile situation, Kershaw somehow suppressed whatever fear he had and performed heroically. Sadly, his bold, unpanicked actions and personal courage in this incident are seldom acknowledged.[15]

In the fall of 1864, Kershaw and his division were heavily involved in the intense fighting at Spotsylvania Court House, Cold Harbor and elsewhere. His division served for a period with General Early in the Shenandoah Valley before returning to the trenches around

Brigadier General Micah Jenkins. *Library of Congress.*

Petersburg. Kershaw was one of six Confederate generals captured at Sailor's Creek on April 6, 1865. Though treated kindly, he was not offered parole but sent to Fort Warren in Boston Harbor, where he remained as a prisoner of war until late July.

Returning to his beloved home of Camden after four years of meritorious service, Kershaw resumed his legal profession. After Reconstruction, he was elected a district judge, a position he held until 1893, when his health began failing. He died peacefully a year later, leaving behind a legacy of military excellence, a highly respected judicial career and devoted service to the Palmetto State.

GENERAL THOMAS M. LOGAN

From Private to General

Over four hundred soldiers in the Confederate army were commissioned as generals. Charlestonian Thomas M. Logan was one of the few among this number who rose from the rank of private. By all accounts, young

Logan was endowed with exceptional abilities that served him well during his entire life.

The son of a judge, Logan graduated first in his class at South Carolina College (now the University of South Carolina) in 1860 and enlisted in the Washington Light Infantry in early 1861. His company became a part of the Hampton Legion Infantry Battalion the following June. It was then that he received his first promotion by being elected second lieutenant. The Hampton Legion distinguished itself at First Manassas in July 1861, and Logan was elected captain of his company shortly afterward. In this capacity, he saw fighting in several major battles in 1862, including the Peninsula Campaign and especially in the Seven Days Battles in June, where he incurred a severe foot wound. He returned to his company in time for the Second Battle of Manassas in August and displayed such gallantry at Sharpsburg in September that he was promoted to major. A month later, he was promoted to lieutenant colonel.

The Hampton Legion Infantry saw no further substantial action until the autumn of 1863, when General James Longstreet took his corps to Georgia. The legion missed the Battle of Chickamauga but was quite active in Longstreet's subsequent engagements at Chattanooga and Knoxville. Logan's abilities were put to good and effective use in this period by leading Longstreet's advance guard and commanding the corps' sharpshooters at each location. His daring and skillful leadership met with Longstreet's approval.

In May 1864, the Hampton Legion Infantry was converted to a cavalry command and placed in Brigadier General Martin Gary's brigade in the Department of Richmond commanded by Lieutenant General Richard Ewell. In this transition, Logan was promoted to colonel, thus succeeding Gary as the Legion's longtime commander. Gary's Brigade was stationed north of the James to protect Richmond and saw a variety of actions over the next several months. It was heavily involved at Riddell's Shop in June, where Logan was wounded in both arms, and again at Nance's Shop ten days later. The brigade provided distinguished service in the October Battle of Williamsburg Road by driving a much larger Union cavalry force from the field and then utterly routing a brigade of U.S. Colored Troops infantry. Logan and the legion were prominent in all these actions.

In December 1864, Matthew Butler was promoted to major general and elevated to division commander. Logan was nominated for brigadier general and to assume command of Butler's old brigade. The nomination failed when Congress did not confirm it, and this is where Logan's body of work over the years was acknowledged and presented to Congress in the most emphatic manner.

A second nomination was submitted with lengthy letters of support from Generals Longstreet, Ewell, Butler and Gary with each attesting to Logan's skill as a commander and to his personal valor. These endorsements, along with wholehearted support from Generals Wade Hampton and Robert E. Lee, led Congress to confirm Logan's appointment as brigadier general on February 15, 1865, just sixteen days short of his twenty-fifth birthday. With this promotion, Logan became the seventh member of the Hampton Legion to be commissioned as a general in the Confederate army.[16]

South Carolina College and Its Confederate Generals

South Carolina College, now the University of South Carolina, admitted its first class in 1809 with just nine students. In the following years, it grew in numbers and established a reputation of being the finest college in the South, drawing students from all across that section of the country. The War for Southern Independence found its graduates serving at all levels in the officer corps of the Confederate army. Twenty-one of them rose to the rank of general.

Perhaps the most prominent and well-known of these generals were cavalrymen. Wade Hampton III (class of 1836) tops this list by rising to lieutenant general. Close behind are three other well-established names. Matthew C. Butler (1856) rose to major general while serving under Hampton in the Army of Northern Virginia. The other two distinguished soldiers, well-known to scholars, come from the Army of Tennessee. John Austin Wharton (1850), a Texan, received a major general's commission for his highly credible service under "Fighting Joe" Wheeler. James R. Chalmers of Mississippi (1851) provided outstanding service as a brigadier general with command of a division under Nathan Bedford Forrest.

There were seventeen other brigadier generals. Maxcy Gregg (1836) would likely have become a major general had he not been mortally wounded at Fredericksburg in 1862. States Rights Gist (1850) was another who carried a superb reputation as a brigade commander but died of wounds received during the Battle of Franklin in November 1864, one of six Confederate generals killed in that action. Samuel McGowan's (1841) chances of being selected as a major general were likely diminished as a result of being wounded several times, causing lengthy absences from duty. Known as a top-notch brigade commander, he needed a cane for walking in the last months of the war. Many historians feel that had Stephen Elliott Jr. (1850) been "discovered" sooner than 1864, he would have likely earned strong consideration for a major general's commission for his special leadership abilities.

Men whose service was quite familiar to wartime South Carolinians and still resonates today include Milledge Bonham (1834), John Bratton (1850), James Connor (1849), John Doby Kennedy (1857), Thomas Logan (1860) and William Henry Wallace (1849). Each served honorably and with distinction.

South Carolina College graduates who earned recognition while leading troops from other states include James Cantey (1837) of Alabama, Daniel Govan (1848) of Arkansas, Henry Gray Jr. (1834) of Louisiana, Louis Wigfall (1837) of Texas, John B. Floyd (1826) of Virginia, John King Jackson (1846) of Georgia and Dandridge McRae (1849) of Alabama. Cantey, Gray and Wigfall were each raised in South Carolina but moved west after graduation. One other man, Thomas Neville Waul (1831), left the college after his junior year and ultimately became a respected brigadier general from Texas.

As a group, these men provided outstanding and faithful service in their leadership roles. Present in many of the major battles of the war, they saw much action in a host of lesser engagements as well. A review of their individual service clearly displays the soldierly qualities justifying their promotions.[17]

Connections to the Confederacy's Medical Department

The advent of war brought men from all sections of life to army enlistment centers. Many of these new soldiers came from the various colleges and private male academies within the state. Furman, Wofford, Erskine, Newberry and South Carolina College lost enrollment and even some professors. The Citadel maintained its battalion-sized enrollment and contributed mightily to the defense of South Carolina, and today's Corps of Cadets proudly carry nine battle streamers earned over the course of the war.

The Medical College of the State of South Carolina (now the Medical University of South Carolina) alumni, professors and students also joined the army, with the vast majority going to the Medical Department. Almost one hundred men are listed in the annals as army surgeons or assistant-surgeons. Two of these men are especially prominent and generally considered the most influential officers in the entire Confederate Army Medical Department.

SAMUEL PRESTON MOORE, a Charleston native and an 1834 graduate of the Medical College of the State of South Carolina, served in the U.S. Army first as an assistant surgeon and later as a surgeon, achieving the rank of major. His service, from 1835 until South Carolina's secession in December 1860, established

Samuel Moore. *Courtesy of the Waring Historical Library, MUSC, Charleston, South Carolina.*

his reputation as a leader in the military medical field and led to an offer by Confederate president Jefferson Davis to become the first acting surgeon general of the Confederate army. Moore accepted the offer on July 30, 1861, and went on to provide badly needed leadership for the Medical Department.

Moore quickly set about organizing the Confederate Medical Department, establishing examination boards for surgeons and assistant surgeons and setting up procurement of hospital and surgical supplies and equipment. Recruiting qualified candidates was intensified under a prescribed guideline. His imprint on the department shows clear, capable and effective planning within the limitations of assets facing the Confederacy.

JULIAN JOHN CHISOLM, born in Charleston in 1830, graduated from the Medical College of the State of South Carolina in 1850. Additional studies in Paris prepared him for his return to Charleston, where he became a premier physician and surgeon. Additionally, he helped open a free hospital for treatment of slaves. When war erupted between Italy and Austria in 1859, Chisolm traveled to Milan to observe treatment of wounded and study military surgery.

Chisolm was in Charleston when Fort Sumter was captured in April 1861. Appointed to the rank of surgeon the following September, he was the first commissioned medical officer from South Carolina and, likely in the entire Confederacy. His early military posts include the South Carolina Hospital in Richmond and other hospitals in Charleston, Columbia and elsewhere. He became adept at setting up hospitals, established a medical purveyor's office and began the first medical laboratories in the Confederacy at Columbia to counter shortage of medicines resulting from the Union blockade.

Early in the war, the surgeon general of the Confederacy tasked him with writing a manual for Confederate surgeons. This publication, published in 1861 and titled *A Manual of Military Surgery, For the Use of Surgeons in the Confederate States of America with an Appendix of the Rules and Regulations of the Medical Department of the Confederate States Army*, was used to train and guide army surgeons. As Chisolm put it in his preface, "Military surgery, which is one of expediency, differs so much from civil practice. The [manual] contains the fruit of European experience, as dearly purchased in recent campaigning."[18] His thinking was far ahead of the time, for he included chapters on food, clothing and hygiene. The manual was recognized as the authority for military surgery and used by surgeons all across the South. His abilities, tireless energy, organizational skills and vast knowledge of military medical needs made him an invaluable asset to the young nation.[19]

Julian John Chisolm. *Courtesy of the Waring Historical Library, MUSC, Charleston, South Carolina.*

PROMOTIONS AND LEADERSHIP IN THE CONFEDERATE ARMY

The Confederacy provided two methods of promotion for soldiers. The first, and most common, was through unit elections. In these, the individual soldiers of a command voted on who would hold which rank. The other method, much more limited, was through the Valor and Skill Act of 1862.

Each was designed to ensure capable leadership from company-level upward through the chain of command.

Companies and regiments from the Palmetto State, like all their Confederate sister states, set up their chain of command by election. Most of those selected at the start of the war were chosen based on community prominence, family ties and personalities. Many men in leadership positions usually lacked any form of military knowledge other than a brief "School of the Soldier" training period or informal militia experience. Some were in their fifties or sixties, and the first battles of the war clearly showed uneven leadership.

In the spring of 1862, with enlistments about to expire, the South sought to make the army stronger as it underwent a massive reorganization. First, it implemented the draft, setting the ages of eighteen to thirty-five. Men older than this age limit were allowed to leave the army. It also allowed men to transfer to other commands while continuing to allow officers and noncommissioned officers (corporals and sergeants) of each command to be set by elections. The need to train officers and enlisted men became a high priority, and steps were taken to ensure highly qualified men were in the right places.

A stronger officer corps was recognized as the focal point of enhancing the army. Officers were expected to study and become intimately familiar with a variety of army training manuals. To ensure the lessons of the manuals and battlefield experience were understood, the army convened examining boards for all levels of promotion and retention. These boards, usually consisting of several senior officers, issued questions on tactics, regulations and other duties applicable to the rank in question. An officer found competent by the board was then able to receive promotion. At the same time, examination boards could find an officer incompetent or disqualified and thereby have his commission revoked. While these boards varied in composition, a typical one might have three colonels examining captains, five captains examining lieutenants and other officers examining NCOs. The boards were also used for instruction and encouragement while making sure those in front of them fully understood the duties expected of them.

Numerous accounts are found confirming the study of military manuals by South Carolinians, officers and enlisted men, alone or in groups. A classic example is Beaufort native Colonel Stephen Elliott, who was tested before being approved for promotion to brigadier general and wrote about studying the training manuals to prepare himself for the new role. Courage was always a factor in promotions, and men who studied their manuals while displaying leadership or courage in battle were usually quickly selected if a position opened. The records are filled with corporals or sergeants with solid backgrounds elevated to officer rank. Their record of success was high at least partly as a result of the preparation for examination board requirements and personal study.

The Confederacy worked hard to acknowledge deeds of heroism and gallantry of its soldiers. Promotion was seen as the best method to do so, and the War Department encouraged company and regimental elections to promote those who had performed valorous deeds. In October 1862, the Valor and Skill Act was passed to allow for promotion from enlisted ranks directly to officer status in recognition of distinguished valor and skill on the battlefield. Officers, too, could receive promotions under the act.

The act was intended not only to honor men for their personal courage but also to place them in a position of leadership and inspiration for others. Nominations were submitted to the War Department by their commanding officers, usually a regimental commander, but occasionally by those much higher in the chain of command, who personally attested to the justification for such a promotion. The caveat was that there must be an open officer's billet in his immediate command for a man to be promoted. The only available list of those promoted under the act was produced in January 1864 and identifies just ninety-two enlisted men promoted to officer rank under this act during the previous year. Of this number, seventy-two were sergeants, four were corporals and sixteen were privates. Men from every Confederate state except Arkansas were included. Virginia led the list with thirty-three named, and Texas was at the bottom with just one. Seven South Carolinians were included. Of these ninety-two men, eighty-three were promoted to second lieutenant and eight others to first lieutenant. One man, a private in the Second Georgia Cavalry, was promoted to captain for, among other things, capturing two Union cannon complete with their crews, horses and accouterments single-handedly at the Battle of Murfreesboro.

Most historians and researchers estimate that perhaps 250 enlisted men at most received promotions in this manner over the course of the war. Others, including a number of South Carolinians, had their nominations held pending open billets that never came. Some soldiers declined to accept promotion to officer's rank. One Virginia private who single-handedly fought off Union attackers trying to capture his cannon declined promotion of any sort because he could not read or write. He still served with distinction and as a source of inspiration to his compatriots. Several were simply uncomfortable with the roles and responsibilities required of officer rank. One of Wade Hampton's Iron Scouts, a sergeant, declined to accept a promotion to captain, for it would have taken him away from scouting.

A small number of officers were promoted under the act as well. Captain J.B. Lyle of the Fifth South Carolina Infantry was promoted to only major for his valor in capturing nearly six hundred Yankees virtually single-handedly because no higher billets were open. Captain B.L. Farinholt of Virginia, however, was advanced to full colonel following his smashing victory at Staunton River Bridge. The Skill and Valor Act of 1862 was a great step in acknowledging heroism. At the same time, it kept the officer corps at a high level of competency and strong leadership.[20]

Yankee Generals and Their Fixation on Fort Sumter

Most histories mention Fort Sumter only as the flash point of the war in April 1861 when it was shelled and captured by Confederate forces. Little attention is given to the fort's later history. Fort Sumter was shelled on 280 different days between August

Fort Sumter before the first great bombardment. *Naval History & Heritage Command.*

1863—when Union operations began in earnest to destroy it and drive the Southern garrison away—and the fall of Charleston. The epic Confederate defense of the fort was absolutely remarkable in every aspect, with countless acts of heroism and superb leadership that should never be ignored or overlooked in the wartime studies of the Palmetto State.

Fort Sumter was strategically placed in Charleston's harbor. Its heavy guns were placed not only to defend against enemy shipping but also capable of defending against enemy troops on nearby Morris Island if necessary. In July 1863, Union land forces under General Quincy Gillmore failed in two attempts to capture Battery Wagner by direct assault. Knowing the key to Union success in capturing all of Morris Island and opening Charleston to attack by the navy lay in the destruction of Fort Sumter, Gillmore mounted a long-range bombardment of Sumter on August 17 with his artillery supported by heavy guns from the Union blockading fleet. The twelve-day bombardment of about 6,800 shells, officially termed the "First Major" bombardment, destroyed the fort as an artillery bastion and raised hopes that the position could be easily taken by force.

However, a small-boat assault by sailors and marines on the night of September 9 was easily repulsed with a loss of about 130 men killed or captured.

Gillmore issued a General Order to his troops on September 15 that read in part:

> *Fort Sumter is destroyed.... The Fort has been in the possession of the enemy for more than two years, has been its pride and boast...has defied the assaults of the most powerful and gallant fleet the world ever saw....Its walls are now crumbled to ruins, its formidable batteries are silenced, and though a hostile flag still floats over it, the fort is a harmless and helpless wreck.*[21]

Union major general Quincy Gillmore. *Library of Congress.*

Fort Sumter being shelled, probably in the second great bombardment. *Library of Congress.*

Gillmore continued shelling Sumter on a random basis to harass the fort's garrison but also mounted the "Second Major" bombardment to destroy the fort's reestablished seaward-facing artillery battery with hopes the garrison would be driven away. Further, he ordered five "Minor" bombardments before he was relieved by Major General John G. Foster and sent, with many of his troops, to Virginia in early May 1864.

Foster was intimately familiar with Fort Sumter. April 1861 found him as a captain among the U.S. officers at Fort Sumter when it was surrendered to Confederate forces. Now in command of U.S. troops around Charleston, he was under strict orders to assume a defensive stance. The U.S. War Department felt it would require sixty thousand men three months to take Charleston, and resources were expected to be stretched in support of the campaigns of Grant in the east and Sherman in the west. Accordingly, Charleston was relegated to a secondary target status. Nevertheless, Foster became intensely fixated on Fort Sumter and set about planning to capture it and perhaps even Charleston.

Foster's viewpoint was that Sumter simply had not been shelled enough. His thinking seems to ignore that the fort had endured nearly 29,000 heavy shells hurled at it in two major and five minor bombardments in less than a year. Shortly after his arrival, he ordered another minor bombardment, one that sent 220 shells at the fort over a period of five days. This was primarily to let his Confederate counterparts know that there would be no change from Gillmore's predilection for shelling and to keep Sumter's garrison from becoming comfortable. Foster ordered another, the "Sixth Minor," a five-day shelling of Sumter on May 13 and the "Seventh Minor" on May 30, a much smaller one but extending over a full week.

His guns then remained silent until July 7, when he unleashed the "Third Great" bombardment. Foster's intentions were to breach and weaken the remaining walls, then bring them down with torpedo rafts exploding close by. In his mind, the Confederate garrison would be forced to evacuate or be captured by a strong follow-up landing force. Over the course of sixty days and nights, heavy Union guns pounded Fort Sumter, firing almost 15,000 shells at the fort. The bombardment ended on September 4 in complete failure. Sumter remained in Confederate hands. Its indomitable engineers worked wonders in keeping abreast of damage, and in the end the

Union major general John G. Foster. *Library of Congress.*

fort was stronger than before. The eighth and final "minor" bombardment of 570 shells from September 6 to 18 closed out the heavy shelling.

Foster was much disappointed at the turn of events. He had exhausted his ammunition supply, and the war department would not send him a replenishment sufficient for his purposes. Additionally, this heavy barrage wore out many of his heavy guns in the midst of the shelling. To get around this, he had to call on the navy to send him a battery of six eleven-inch guns complete with officers, crew and ammunition to supplement his bombardment. With a limited ammunition capability, Union guns could do no more than fire intermittently at the fort until Charleston's evacuation in February 1865.

From August 1863 until its evacuation, Sumter was targeted by an estimated 47,000 heavy shells weighing approximately 3,500 tons (7 million pounds). Successfully withstanding this unparalleled shelling was an astonishing achievement properly acknowledged by the *Confederate Defenders* monument on Charleston's Battery.

Union Bombardments of Fort Sumter

Number and Class	Dates	Approximate # of Shells Fired
First Major	8/17–9/2/1863	6,800
First Minor	9/28–10/3/1863	570
Second Major	10/26–12/6/1863	18,000
Second Minor	12/11/1863	220
Third Minor	1/28–1/31/1864	600
Fourth Minor	3/15/1864	140
Fifth Minor	4/28–5/4/1864	510
Sixth Minor	5/13–5/17/1864	1,150
Seventh Minor	5/30–6/5/1864	220
Third Major	7/7–9/3/1864	14,800
Eighth Minor	9/6–9/18/1864	570

ESTIMATED TOTAL OF SHELLS Fired at Fort Sumter during these Bombardments: 43,380. Approximately 3,700 more were in a desultory manner from August 1863 until the fall of Charleston in February 1865. All figures from the National Park Service Fort Sumter and Fort Moultrie locations and brochures.

FORT SUMTER'S RESOLUTE COMMANDER, MAJOR STEPHEN ELLIOTT

General Stephen Elliott was one of South Carolina's most respected figures during the war, and his path to the rank of general is far different than that of any other. Unfortunately, his name recognition has dropped significantly since the Centennial of the 1960s, leading to his valor and leadership being overlooked by many. This article, a summary of his military service, is meant to reintroduce him to students and historians alike and bring him and his accomplishments back into the forefront. South Carolina's wartime history without mention of Stephen Elliott would be far from complete.

STEPHEN ELLIOTT WAS A rising star in his hometown of Beaufort when South Carolina seceded from the Union in December 1860. At age thirty, he was a graduate of South Carolina College, an attorney, a planter and a member of the South Carolina House of Representatives. Additionally, he served as captain of the famed Beaufort Volunteer Artillery. His passions, though, were sailing and fishing.

Elliott's knowledge of the waters in and around Port Royal Sound were well documented. In May 1861, Elliott was pilot for the Confederate gunboat *Lady Davis*, which sought to battle a U.S. warship reported to be lurking off the coast. Though the warship wasn't found, a U.S.-flagged merchantman, the *A.B. Thompson*, was taken as the first war prize of either side.

In June 1861, he and his battery were sent to Bay Point Island at the mouth of Port Royal Sound. There, Captain Elliott was instrumental in construction of Fort Beauregard by demonstrating natural engineering skills while serving simultaneously as fort commander and ordnance officer. His performance in the November 1861 Battle of Port Royal received high praise from senior commanders, and his men gave him a handsome presentation sword afterward.

A day after that battle, General Robert E. Lee arrived in South Carolina as department commander with his headquarters based in Coosawhatchie until recalled to Richmond in March 1862. During this period, Elliott was called on by Lee on several occasions "for performance of special duty in which he showed good judgement, and exhibited intelligence, boldness and sagacity."[22] Additionally, until June 1863, Elliott led a number of waterborne raids against Union outposts around Port Royal Sound. These raids, described as "frequent, daring and resourceful," led to him being described "as much a sailor as soldier."[23] A raid on Pinckney Island in which nearly all fifty-seven Yankees posted there were killed or captured earned national attention. Another headlined action was when he and his artillery ambushed and sank a U.S. Navy gunboat. Elliott displayed great personal valor in the October 1862 Battle of Pocotaligo, skillfully placing and directing his artillery, which led to his promotion to major of artillery.

Elliott was transferred to the Torpedo Department at Charleston in July 1863. In August, Fort Sumter was pounded into ruins and rubble by heavy rifled Union guns from nearby Morris Island and the Union fleet. The shelling, termed the "First Great Bombardment," dismounted and/or covered in rubble thirty-nine of the fort's forty cannon. With Sumter no longer a viable artillery bastion, General P.G.T. Beauregard ignored suggestions to abandon it and chose to garrison it as an infantry post. Beauregard handpicked Major Elliott to command the fort despite having an abundance of available infantry officers.

Confederate brigadier general Stephen Elliott. *Library of Congress*.

Elliott took command of Fort Sumter on September 4, 1863, under the most difficult circumstances. Ordered to defend and hold Sumter to the last extremity, he faced a myriad of challenges and privations. For the next four months, he and his superb engineers vastly improved the fort's defenses and living conditions. At the same time, his vigilance resulted in a stunning defeat of a Union small boat assault and deterred others. Additionally, he was able to mount a three-gun battery facing the harbor entrance.

Union general Quincy Gillmore, commanding U.S. troops around Charleston, heard of the progress at Sumter and initiated the "Second Great Bombardment" of Sumter. From October 26 through December 5, 1863, Gillmore's guns fired nearly nineteen thousand heavy shells at Sumter in a futile attempt to deliver fatal blows to the fort's progress and drive Elliott and his garrison away or wipe it out. Elliott's resolve and ability to continue his progress on the fort so impressed Confederate president Jefferson Davis that he issued an executive order promoting Elliott to lieutenant colonel of artillery. Gillmore was equally impressed with Elliott's work and emphatically demonstrated his respect on New Year's Eve 1863. When Sumter's evening colors gun sounded that day, Gillmore had the U.S. flag on Morris Island "dipped" in formal salute to the fort and its resolute commander.[24]

Elliott's eight-month command of Sumter exceeded all hopes. The fort remained in Confederate hands, and six guns were remounted despite having almost twenty-two thousand Union shells hurled at it. In early May 1864, he was promoted to colonel in command of the Holcombe Legion Infantry and sent to Virginia. Following the loss of his brigade commander on May 20, Elliott was promoted to brigadier general and given command of the brigade five days later after having been a colonel less than a month.

General Elliott performed commendably in severe action at Petersburg in June and July 1864. However, Union forces exploded four tons of black powder under his position on July 30, kicking off the Battle of the Crater. While preparing his command to meet the Union threat, he was hit by a bullet that passed through his left arm, penetrated his chest and lodged in his lung. Medically furloughed through the end of the year while his wounds healed, Elliott never regained use of his arm.

Elliott cut his furlough short to command a heavy artillery brigade near Charleston in early December. His physical condition was still frail when Charleston was evacuated on February 17, 1865, and his senior officers had concerns that the long marches ahead might be too difficult for him. Declining two opportunities to relinquish his command, an action that would have been free of criticism, Elliott chose to stay with his men. He led his brigade well over the next two months while fighting as infantry at Averasboro and again at Bentonville, where he received his fifth wound of the war.

When the army was surrendered and paroled at Durham Station in April 1865, Elliott returned to Beaufort, only to find his property had been seized by the U.S. government. Further, his rights and privileges as a citizen were forfeited under a directive by U.S. president Andrew Johnson. Forced to live in a seaside fishing hut, he earned a meager living by fishing and selling his catch despite having just one good arm. After two attempts to regain citizenship failed, Elliott appealed to his old foe from Fort Sumter days, Union general Quincy Gillmore, now stationed at nearby Hilton head, for intervention. To Gillmore's everlasting credit, his personal letter on behalf of Elliott to President Johnson resulted in Elliott's citizenship being quickly restored. Unfortunately, Elliott was unable to recover his property.

Stephen Elliott died in February 1866. His death was attributed to the wounds received from the Crater and his physical exertions afterward. Among the many tributes that followed is one often overlooked. The very first chartered United Confederate Veterans camp in South Carolina, no. 51 in St. George, formed as the "Stephen Elliott Camp," a fitting tribute to a South Carolina legend and hero.[25]

4

BLOCKADE OF SOUTH CAROLINA'S COAST

The Union blockade of Southern ports has been heavily researched and studied by many prominent historians. However, the wartime blockade of South Carolina's coast is usually incompletely presented. Blockade runners operating in stealthy secrecy left little in the form of documentation, but other available sources provide clear glimpses into this clandestine activity. Unfortunately, many historians and scholars whose work is beyond reproach otherwise barely touch on South Carolina's bustling and vibrant blockade running of 1861 to mid-1862. Further, their studies usually focus only on Charleston, thereby neglecting aspects crucial to understanding the entire blockade-running picture, which stretched the entire length of South Carolina's coast. Equally important, the military efforts of the Confederate army and navy to counter the blockade are often ignored despite being a critical aspect of blockade-running endeavors. This chapter is intended to give a brief overview of these closely intertwined topics.

In April 1861, Abraham Lincoln declared a blockade of the entire Southern coast stretching from Virginia to Texas, a total of 3,500 miles, with intentions of severing commercial ties between the South and the rest of the world. South Carolina had 187 of those miles, and Charleston was one of largest and most active ports in the South. In addition to a fine harbor, the city had crucial railroad connections running north, south and west. Georgetown and Beaufort were also active ports but lacked railroad connections.

Charleston was the Confederacy's primary blockade running port until Morris Island was taken by Union forces in September 1863. But from the war's earliest days until its end in 1865, smaller locations between Charleston and the North Carolina line were actively engaged in this business. McClellanville, Winyah Bay, Murrells Inlet, the North and South Edisto Rivers, the North and South Santee Rivers and Little River were constantly receiving and sending smaller merchant ships full of trade goods. On occasion, the Combahee River and Pawley's Island saw such activity. These sites utilized wagons, lighters and, in some locations, tugs to shuttle cargo between the ships, plantations, mills and communities well inland. Little River and Murrells Inlet had such an abundance of shipping trade that wharves and warehouse were built to properly handle it all. These well-coordinated activities were sizeable in numbers and quantities.

For generations, the economy of Horry County was built around the exportation of naval stores. Lumber, rosin, tar and turpentine were key products needed for shipbuilding and maintenance. These same commodities were an integral part of Georgetown County's economy as well. Such trade required smaller shallow-draft ships to safely navigate the waters and rivers. Ships could enter Winyah Bay and sail up the Waccamaw River inland almost to Conway. Both the North and South Santee Rivers allowed safe navigation for many miles upstream. In summary, all the sites north of Charleston were well established ports of call before the war and continued their ways throughout it.

Lincoln and the U.S. Navy quickly learned it was one thing to proclaim a blockade but quite another to enforce it. It took over a year for the navy to obtain sufficient ships for a significant effect on blockade running. Meanwhile, innovative and daring entrepreneurs in South Carolina, the British Isles and elsewhere continued a highly active and productive trade. Sailing ships of all sorts—brigs, brigantines, sloops, barks and especially schooners—left various sites in the Palmetto State laden with turpentine, tobacco, rice, rosin and, occasionally, peanuts. Those returning from England carried a wide assortment of commodities primarily for personal, household or industrial use along with limited quantities of military goods. Other vessels sailed to ports in the Caribbean with turpentine, rosin and rice and returned loaded with fresh fruit, sugar, soda, candles, fish, tea, coffee, salt and molasses.

Cotton exports were quite limited until late 1862 but later rose to become the top Southern export. Sizeable import shipments of arms, munitions and other commodities needed by the military began arriving in mid-1861 and became the top import as the war continued leaving less room for personal commodities. Military cargo landed in Wilmington, North

Carolina, went almost exclusively to Richmond for distribution to the Army of Northern Virginia. Though some of it landing in Charleston was shipped to Richmond, the vast majority went to Augusta, Georgia, to support the Army of Tennessee.

By late 1861, British and Confederate interests had begun using Nassau, Bermuda and Havana as trans-shipment points for economic efficiency. Vessels with cargo for the Confederacy sailed to these ports to have their contents offloaded and placed on a blockade runner destined for a Southern port. In turn, export goods from Southern states received at these ports were placed on ships destined for the British Isles or elsewhere. South Carolina's coastal shipping points used Nassau, just a two-day transit, as their principal trans-shipment point.

Mid-1862 found the Union navy strength sufficient to ensure a closer blockade, and with many fast new steamers within this enlarged fleet, the days of sailing ship blockade runners were numbered. However, blockade runners anticipated these events and switched from sail to steam without skipping a beat.

Transits were full of danger and suspense for the blockade runners. Despite these vessels flying flags of neutral nations, international law allowed Union warships to stop them on the high seas. They then had their manifests and other documents closely examined for irregularities and were searched for contraband. Yankee boarding officers often seized a ship if any suspicion at all was raised, and numerous blockade runners were taken in this fashion. Danger was always present as a vessel made its final dash to or departure from South Carolina's harbors. Some were intercepted and captured while others were driven ashore by alert Union vessels, yet the overwhelming majority of transits were successful.

The U.S. Navy was challenged to maintain a blockade. Its ships had to return to port for regular maintenance, coal and other supplies or for

Sketch of Union blockading fleet at Charleston. *Naval History & Heritage Command.*

repairs incurred from damage by the many storms they encountered. The primary base supporting the blockading squadron off South Carolina was Beaufort, captured in November 1861. In short, one-third of the Union ships were on station at any one time with another third at Beaufort and the other third in transit to or from their station. Additionally, these warships were routinely taken off station to support army activities or raids all along the coast of South Carolina, Georgia or Florida. As a result, only Charleston had permanent blockading presence while South Carolina's other smaller port sites faced only intermittent Union navy presence.

The Union blockade of Charleston in late 1862 was becoming more effective as more ships, especially steamers, were added to the fleet. In January 1863, Confederate general P.G.T. Beauregard sent the new ironclads CSS *Palmetto State* and CSS *Chicora* against the blockading fleet off Charleston to break the blockade. If the enemy could be driven away for a day, then Charleston and all other Southern ports could be declared open again and Lincoln would have to give formal notice to the world again before he could impose another blockade. Depending on events, that might require a period as long as sixty days in which no merchant ship entering or leaving a Southern port could be molested.

Beauregard's plan worked to perfection. The Union fleet was surprised, beaten and dispersed by the Confederate ironclads and disappeared over the

Confederate gunboat CSS *Palmetto State. Library of Congress.*

horizon not to return for well over twenty-four hours. British, French and Spanish consuls in Charleston confirmed the situation to their governments, expecting, under international law, for the blockade to be declared broken. However, a major international kerfuffle erupted from Lincoln's refusal to acknowledge the blockade was broken. In the end, there was little the European nations could do to counter this egregious violation of international law and Beauregard's success came to naught.[26]

While the sortie of the Confederate ironclads failed to break the blockade, it certainly cracked it. Fearful of future attacks, Union warships moved much farther away from Charleston at night, thereby loosening their stranglehold on the port's shipping lanes. This resulted in blockade runners more than doubling their transits. The first eight months of 1863 were the heyday for steamer blockade runners calling at South Carolina locations, with about one hundred successful transits recorded just for Charleston. Service at coastal sites above and below Charleston continued at high levels.

In early September 1863, the Union army did what its navy could not by bringing blockade running at Charleston to a screeching halt through the capture of Morris Island. For six months, until March 1864, not a single blockade runner arrived at or sailed from Charleston. Shipments normally destined there were diverted to Wilmington. Though other blockade running locations along South Carolina's remained open, the South's busiest port was absolutely closed.

During those grueling months of shutdown, General Beauregard and other Confederate leaders sought ways to open the port again. With limited assets and choices, their eyes fell on the spar-torpedo boats, and with Beauregard's personal guidance and encouragement, these new weapons were brought to the forefront.

The first use of this revolutionary type of vessel occurred in August 1863 when the CSS *Torch*, in an unsuccessful attempt to relieve pressure on Battery Wagner, came within a whisker of damaging or sinking the powerful USS *New Ironsides*. The venture, however, was partly successful in that it showed clearly that such an attack was feasible. Another torpedo boat attack was successfully carried out two months later by the *David*, resulting in heavy damage to the *New Ironsides*. On the night of February 17, 1864, the *H.L. Hunley* sank the USS *Housatonic* off Charleston's harbor in the first successful submarine attack in history.

Two other *David* attacks shortly after the *Housatonic* was sunk added further to the Yankee concerns. One, against the USS *Memphis* near the

USS *Housatonic*, sunk by the *H.L. Hunley*. *Naval History & Heritage Command*.

Edisto River on March 6 failed only because the torpedo malfunctioned. The other, against the USS *Wabash* off Charleston on April 18, was foiled when the *Wabash* detected the *David*, slipped anchor and steamed away at high speed. Each of these torpedo boat attacks had a significant effect on the Union fleet. Fear replaced complacency in the minds of officers and crew of the blockaders and they moved farther and farther away from Charleston at night.

March and April 1864 saw small numbers of blockade runners returning to discover Charleston was again open to them. With the Union fleet no longer positioned so tightly, they slipped past Union blockaders and the guns on Morris Island into or from Charleston's harbor. The port began a gradual increase in blockade running transits, and the last half of 1864 surged to levels reached before Morris Island fell a year earlier. That growth continued right up to Charleston's evacuation in February 1865.

Those unnamed and unsung individuals handling blockade running operations at McClellanville, Murrells Inlet, Georgetown, the North and South Santee Rivers and Little River Inlet as well as those on the North and South Edisto Rivers performed brilliantly throughout the war and deserve credit and recognition. Most were targeted by the Union navy multiple times over the course of the war. While permanent blockading of these sites was not possible, each received substantial attention in the form of offshore shelling or via assault by sailors and marines landing

Union warship USS *Wabash*, a blockader targeted by the *Little David* spar-torpedo boat in 1864. *Naval History & Heritage Command.*

from ship's launches as early as May 1862. Georgetown and Little River were targeted frequently, but Murrells Inlet received the brunt of attention all through the war. In April 1863, a Union shelling and raid on Murrells Inlet resulted in one blockade runner and two warehouses destroyed. Two weeks later, the Union navy returned again, destroying another blockade runner and damaging four others. Upstream sites along the Waccamaw and Santee Rivers were raided by warships but found no shipping operations. Blockade running operators everywhere showed great resilience and maintained their operations. Just a single event involving the Combahee River is known and occurred in January 1865 when a blockade runner was captured well upriver.

Most authoritative studies conclude that the overall Union blockade of the Southern coast was a failure and generally ineffective while estimating that as much as 90 percent of blockade running transits were successful. Although no specific figures are available, South Carolina's blockade running efforts were probably at least at that level. Blockade running was indeed, as one prominent historian wrote, the lifeline of the Confederacy. It is certain that Charleston had a big hand in this, but the other shipping sites along coastal South Carolina deserve recognition as well.[27]

5

NAVAL OPERATIONS

1861–1865

CHALLENGES FACING THE UNION FLEET

The start of the war found the U.S. Navy with 42 active vessels and 48 others in reserve. Nearly all were sailing ships. The navy began the process of enlarging its fleet and by war's end had 671 active ships. Many of those, however, were designed exclusively for inland river duties and never saw ocean service. Some of the newer ships were fast, light-draft sloops carrying ten to twenty guns while a few were much larger and with as many fifty guns. Additionally, the navy built the *Monitor* and other ironclad-type vessels carrying massive guns. Together, it was a formidable fleet with multiple capabilities. Yet it had drawbacks.

The guiding principle was that success against Confederate forts required at least a 15:1 advantage in guns. The difficulty of hitting targets from a vessel in constant motion from influence of wind and sea is apparent, and the only way to counter this was to have overwhelming firepower, requiring many ships. This worked well against Confederate forts at Cape Hatteras, Port Royal and elsewhere but not Charleston. The navy's huge guns did not have to hit Confederate guns to be considered effective. Having the bursting shells inflict casualties on Confederate gun crews or drive them away from their posts were immediate goals. Creating disruptions and destruction within a fort's interior was expected to bring fear to the defenders and diminish their determination to fight. These "in the vicinity" shelling tactics worked especially well when the vessels could fire at ranges longer than those of the fort's smaller weaponry.

The *Monitor*-class vessels provided little in the overall operations against Charleston. Sent to Charleston to deter sorties by the Confederate ironclads, they were hopelessly inept and outgunned in their ill-fated attempt to force their way into the harbor in April 1863 for the purpose of destroying Forts Moultrie and Sumter. Taking five minutes or longer to reload each of their guns, they managed to fire about 150 rounds in the battle while being subjected to 2,200 shots, of which over 500 were hits. Five of the attacking ironclads and monitors were heavily damaged, and one sank the next day from battle damage.

Charleston posed a number of problems that were never overcome. The Union navy was stymied by island barriers, shoals and shallow channel waters at low tides. Harbor defenses, buttressed by torpedoes and powerful ironclads, presented strong deterrents, and its largest warships carried drafts too deep to operate in battle within the restricted harbor confines. Wooden vessels were subject to being quickly sunk if they approached too closely. The only location the U.S. Navy could mass its heavy firepower was against Battery Wagner on Morris Island in the summer of 1863. Yet that alone didn't lead to success. It still took determined efforts of the Union army to achieve victory.

The U.S. Navy encountered many difficulties off Charleston. Confederate ironclads *Palmetto State* and *Chicora* showed their prowess by prevailing over several wooden blockading vessels in January 1863. Additionally, two other monitors were lost at Charleston before the war's end. *New Ironsides* was badly damaged by the *Little David*, and the *Housatonic* was sunk by the *H.L. Hunley*. Other vessels, damaged in storms or by scraping shoals, suffered lengthy periods of unavailability. In summary, the U.S. Navy mounted an intense but relatively ineffective blockade. However, it supported the army credibly in a variety of coastal movements.[28]

CSS Juno

And Its Moment of Glory

In early August 1863, Charleston's attention was focused on Battery Wagner, the target of the Union army on Morris Island since early July. With the

Union fleet tightening its blockade of Charleston, there was much to be concerned about, and the news seemed to grow gloomier by the day. However, the night of August 5 saw an action near Charleston's harbor entrance that brought momentary joy and gave the Confederate navy some bragging rights. The action did not involve any of the Union monitors or ironclads, nor did it include any of the powerful Confederate ironclad gunboats. The participants were a large Union navy launch armed with a twelve-pound howitzer carrying a crew of twenty-three and a small Confederate steamer without deck guns.

The CSS *Juno* was a small vessel, an iron-framed paddle-wheeler just sixty-five feet in length but possessing good speed. Built in England as the *Helen*, it was used as an English mail packet until purchased by the Confederate government for use as a blockade runner in May 1863 and renamed the *Juno*.

Evading the Union blockading fleet on its first blockade-running attempt, *Juno* arrived in Charleston on July 8, 1863, from Nassau. Confederate authorities in Charleston, in the midst of the lengthy and ongoing fight on Morris Island, immediately began using *Juno* as a flag of truce vessel, dispatch boat and picket boat. With the threat to Charleston and Fort Sumter increasing daily, *Juno* was soon outfitted with a spar plus a sixty-five-pound torpedo on its bow for use against any enemy vessel it might encounter. Additionally, it carried a bale of cotton affixed to the bow to act as a fender if it had to ram an enemy vessel. *Juno* had no other armament except a few small arms among the crew of just eleven men, including its commander, Lieutenant Philip Porcher (pronounced Por-shay). A Charleston native, Porcher enjoyed a fine reputation as a naval officer and had seen combat previously. He commanded the bow gun on the CSS *Palmetto State* in the ironclad attack on the blockading fleet the previous January and was said to have served throughout the engagement with an unlit cigar between his teeth.

On the night of August 5, 1863, the Union navy moved several monitors close to Fort Sumter and Cummings Point to provide security to the army on Morris Island. Additionally, several large naval launches with crews of twenty to twenty-five men and armed with twelve-pound howitzers were sent even closer to act as picket boats. Their orders were to provide early warning of any Confederate steamers attempting to leave the harbor and to fire on and sink them if possible. One of these launches was from the powerful U.S. frigate *Wabash*, commanded by Acting Masters Mate Edward L. Haines, who received his orders directly from Admiral John Dahlgren, commander of the South Atlantic Blockading Squadron.

That same night, the Confederate gunboat *Chicora* and *Juno* moved to positions off Fort Sumter. Porcher's orders were "run into and sink or capture any of the enemy's barges or launches that came his way."[29] Shortly after midnight, *Juno* started its engines and began moving farther out to reconnoiter the patrol area when it was spotted by the Union launch, which immediately fired and issued a demand to surrender. Lieutenant Porcher showed no inclination to surrender and headed the *Juno* directly toward the launch. The launch fired another shot from its howitzer before realizing the small steamer was intent on running it over. Just prior to the collision, ten of the launch's crew dived overboard.

Juno's engineer in charge, James H. Tomb, reported that after being fired on, "We immediately headed toward her, striking her amidships; but not having much headway on the *Juno*, the launch swung around to port." The launch's commander attempted to recover from the heavy collision and the disaster facing him by leading his remaining crew onto the *Juno* with intentions of capturing the Confederate vessel. Perhaps Porcher had anticipated this, for a call was made throughout the *Juno* for all hands to come topside to repel boarders. Tomb's report continued, "All the engineer division with the balance of the crew fired upon them as they came across the rail. The officer in charge surrendered. As he came over the rail, he had his sword in one hand and one of his boots in the other." Following Haines's lead, the other Union sailors surrendered; all were quickly taken aft, and the launch was secured to the *Juno*.[30]

Thoughts of rescuing the enemy sailors in the water were quickly dashed by the presence of a nearby Union monitor, and the *Juno* returned to the *Chicora* to transfer the thirteen prisoners aboard. Eight of the ten Union sailors who went into the water before the collision were rescued afterward by another Union vessel. Two others swam to Sullivan's Island over two miles away only to be captured the next morning.

The eight men rescued each attested that they had been fired on by *Juno*'s crew while in the water. Admiral Dahlgren quickly filed a protest with Confederate general Beauregard and, shortly afterward, received a denial that such action had occurred. Nevertheless, there were repercussions later on.

Master's Mate Haines, after enduring thirteen months as a prisoner of war before being exchanged, wrote an official report of the incident to U.S. Secretary of the Navy Gideon Welles. He stated the *Juno* was "manned by a crew of 50 men and protected outside and in by cotton bales."[31] Aside from these exaggerations, his report is similar to what is found in other sources.

That not a man was shot, killed or seriously hurt in this short but intense and decisive action is almost miraculous. Strong and aggressive leadership throughout the affair is obvious and reflects credibly on each commander. The call by Porcher for his engineers to come topside for anticipated close-quarters action shows the desperate circumstances and danger facing him. Charleston's newspapers covered this story well and in a prominent manner. The *Daily Courier* headlined it with "Brilliant Naval Exploit" and provided a detailed account of the affair.

One rarely noticed point of interest to researchers and historians is that *Juno*'s capture of the Union launch was the first combat action of a spar-torpedo boat at Charleston. The shallow draft of the launch and the overall circumstances precluded the use of its spar-torpedo, but had a larger Union vessel been encountered that night, *Juno* would have had the historic opportunity of carrying out the first such attack.

The *Juno* continued its multi-role service but was the center of a serious matter a month later. While *Juno* was sailing as a flag of truce vessel, Union guns fired on it without warning. General Beauregard vehemently protested such action in several letters to Admiral Dahlgren, whose explanation, if any was ever issued, has not been found. The affair was almost certainly triggered by the charge that the *Juno* had fired on helpless Union sailors in the water when it captured the launch.

Juno remained in Charleston performing a multitude of roles until early 1864. The port of Charleston had been effectively closed to blockade runners since the fall of Morris Island in September 1863, allowing the Union fleet to tighten its blockade so closely that it was impossible for a runner to enter or depart. That all changed, however, in February 1864 with the sinking of the USS *Housatonic* by the spar-torpedo boat *Hunley* in the world's first successful submarine attack. The Union navy, faced with the threat of further such attacks, was forced to loosen its blockade substantially.

Seeing the opportunity to resume blockade running again, the *Juno* was released from naval duties and was designated to resume its role as a blockade runner under the original name *Helen*. On March 9, 1864, the *Helen*, carrying 220 bales of cotton and still commanded by Lieutenant Porcher, became the first vessel to depart Charleston in six months. It slipped out of Charleston destined for Nassau and made its way safely through the Union blockade. Unfortunately, the next day, *Helen* encountered a gale that broke the vessel apart, and twenty-eight of the thirty men aboard, including Porcher, were lost.

CSS Torch

Charleston's First Torpedo Boat

Historians have long written about the *Little David* and the *Hunley*, but few mention CSS *Torch*, which carried out the very first torpedo boat attack. Its story is found in fragments, leaving much about its origins and final disposition in mystery. Still, what is found adds another chapter in the defense of Charleston.

The *Torch* was built in mid-1863. A small version of an ironclad, it sat low in the water and carried no armor plating or guns. The boat's key feature was that it had "a spar with three branches at the end," each with two one-hundred-pound torpedoes attached. *Torch* was probably rushed into completion, as reports state it leaked badly, had a secondhand engine and exhibited other problems. However, the situation on Morris Island presented an urgent need for *Torch*'s service. With Union guns from the navy and army pounding Battery Wagner at will, General P.G.T. Beauregard anxiously sought some way to relieve the pressure from that position. Accordingly, *Torch* undertook its one and only wartime mission on the night of August 20–21, 1863.

Sailing with an all-volunteer crew under command of Captain James Carlin, *Torch* carried twelve men of the First South Carolina Artillery armed with muskets for defense if Union boats tried to board. Their target was the USS *New Ironsides*, an armored vessel with eighteen heavy guns and a crew of about 450 men. Sinking *New Ironsides* would force the Union navy to cease, or least pause, shelling Battery Wagner.

Captain Carlin found *New Ironsides* off Morris Island with a monitor nearby and determined to go after it once the attack on *New Ironsides* was completed. *Torch* quickly closed on the big ironclad with its spar lowered when, within forty yards of the Union warship, it suffered short failures of both its steering and engine. Unable to steer and without propulsion, *Torch* drifted tantalizingly close past its intended target with Captain Carlin fearing entanglement in the ship's anchor chains. However, *New Ironsides* reacted to the threat by slipping anchor and backing astern to open the distance from *Torch*. On regaining power and steering, Carlin aborted the attack after being fired on by *New Ironsides*.

The mission was unsuccessful, but it showed that the Union navy was susceptible to torpedo boat attacks and set the example for later attempts by other vessels. *Torch* came within perhaps thirty seconds of achieving

Union blockader USS *New Ironsides*. *Naval History & Heritage Command.*

success and lasting fame in its only mission. It remained in service at least into 1864, possibly as an anchored floating battery in Charleston harbor. The courage displayed by those serving on *Torch* that fateful night should not be lost to memory.[32]

UNION SHIPS FIND DANGER IN SOUTH CAROLINA'S WATERS

Union vessels from both navy and army, both sail and steam-powered, cruised the coastal waters and rivers of the Palmetto State during the war. Large, heavily armed warships, fast sloops and ironclads lurked around Charleston. Small shallow-draft gunboats made inland forays via the various rivers. Supporting this fleet were transports, large and small, capable of carrying men, livestock and supplies. Twelve vessels were sunk by Confederate gunfire or storms, one was captured and many others incurred major damage.

The earliest recorded losses are from the Port Royal Expedition destined for Beaufort from Norfolk. They occurred November 2, 1861, when a gale wreaked havoc on it. The transport *Governor*, carrying a battalion of marines, foundered just off Charleston. Somehow, all but seven men were rescued.

Peerless, a transport loaded with beef cattle, foundered very near Charleston's harbor without loss of crewmen. Another transport carrying cattle, barrels of potatoes and other supplies, *Osceola*, foundered off Georgetown, and two boatloads of survivors were captured.

The year 1863 was disastrous for the Union fleet. On January 30, the gunboat *Isaac Smith* became the only warship captured by land forces after sailing into a well-coordinated ambush by Confederate batteries on Charleston's Stono River. The very next day, Union blockaders were routed when Confederate ironclads *Palmetto State* and *Chicora* emerged from early morning darkness and fog intent on breaking the Union blockade. Though no blockaders were sunk, Union warships *Mercedita*, *Keystone State*, *Augusta* and *Quaker State* were damaged in the ensuing engagement.

It got worse as the year went on. The ironclad *Keokuk* sustained such battle damage during the ironclad attack in Charleston Harbor on April 7 that it sank off Morris Island the next day. On April 9, Confederate guns along Whale Branch River near Beaufort ambushed and destroyed Union army gunboat *George Washington*. The October 5 spar-torpedo attack by the *Little David* inflicted much damage to the warship *New Ironsides*. On December 6, a gale sank ironclad *Weehawken* off Morris Island with a loss of thirty-one men.

Just three Union ships were lost in 1864. The *Housatonic*, sunk by the *Hunley* on February 17, was the most notable, as it was the target of the world's first successful submarine attack. On May 26, a Union expedition to cut the Charleston and Savannah Railroad was stopped when the transport *Boston*, loaded with troops and horses ran aground on the Ashepoo River. Blasted by Confederate artillery, it burned to the waterline after being set afire by the crew as they abandoned ship. A gale on December 9 sank the schooner coal-ship and lightship *Robert B. Howlett* off Morris Island.

Three more Union vessels were lost in just a six-week period of 1865. Ironclad *Patapsco* sank a minute after hitting a mine in Charleston Harbor on January 15. The warship *Dai Ching* ran aground on January 26 in the Combahee River near Beaufort, and as the crew abandoned ship after being raked by Confederate guns, they set it afire. The last ship lost was the *Harvest Moon*, which sank on February 2 after hitting a torpedo in Georgetown's harbor.

THE BATTLE OF CHAPMAN'S FORT

May 26, 1864

The Charleston and Savannah Railroad was targeted by Union commanders several times during the war. This vital connection remained open until late December 1864 primarily due to valorous stands by vastly outnumbered Confederate forces possessing superb leadership. The well-documented battles at Pocotaligo in 1862 and Honey Hill and Tulifinny in late 1864, were especially decisive.

The Battle of Chapman's Fort, though well documented, is rarely mentioned. Chapman's Fort was among several unfinished and unmanned positions established in early 1864 along the Ashepoo River and adjacent areas to thwart Union waterborne forays against the interior. The action there in May 1864 can hardly be called a battle, but it halted a threat to the railroad just a few miles away.

In May 1864, Union commanders at Hilton Head assembled a well-equipped two-thousand-man force of infantry, artillery, cavalry and marines at Port Royal with orders to destroy "the railroad bridges over the South Edisto and Ashepoo Rivers and the long trestle-work over the swamp between the two rivers." Loaded on transports accompanied by gunboats, the force sailed on May 25 with intentions of landing the troops during the night.

Somehow, in the darkness, two vessels, one being the army transport *Boston* loaded with horses and a large contingent of U.S. Colored Troops, missed the channel from the river leading to the planned landing site. They continued upstream seven miles before the *Boston* ran aground three hundred yards from Chapman's Fort. Alert scouts reported this, and before daylight, a small Confederate force from the First South Carolina Cavalry and two cannon from Earle's Light Artillery Battery arrived.

The cannon opened fire on *Boston* and immediately hit the boiler. The ship's crew and the USCTs quickly abandoned ship and floundered in the marsh, unable to do more than watch as *Boston* was raked by the shelling. The ship was hit repeatedly over the next couple of hours before arrival of Union gunboats prompted the Confederate guns to cease fire.

A Union gunboat commander wrote in his after-action report that, on arrival at the scene, he found "nearly all the troops ashore in the marsh having thrown away their arms and accouterments, and in many instances their clothing." After all firing ceased and rescue boats were dispatched, the report added, "The colored troops being in a position they could not return the fire, seemed to have been panic-stricken, and…it was as much as the officers could do to keep them from crowding into the boats and swamping them."

The Yankees did not linger at Chapman's Fort but quickly set the *Boston*'s hulk afire without attempting to first recover any of the eighty-five horses still aboard. Thirteen men were reported drowned or missing from the contingent aboard. This disaster led the commanding officer to abort the entire mission and issued orders to return to Port Royal. Anger and disgust with this debacle are evident within the Union post-action reports. The Battle of Chapman's Fort kept the Charleston and Savannah Railroad safe, and it was another two months before the Yankees mounted another (failed) attempt to sever it.[33]

Demise of the USS Dai Ching

The USS *Dai Ching*, a Union gunboat originally built in New York for the emperor of China, was purchased by the U.S. Navy in April 1863 and soon became a fixture in South Carolina's coastal waters and rivers as part of the South Atlantic Blockading Squadron. It shelled Fort Sumter, Battery Wagner and other Confederate positions in Charleston's harbor in the summer of 1863. Armed with two twenty pounders and a one hundred pounder, she had formidable firepower. However, its service ended on January 26, 1865, in perhaps the most shameful and dishonorable affair suffered by the U.S. Navy during the war.

The navy, in support of General W.T. Sherman's early advance into South Carolina, sent gunboats up the Ashepoo, Stono, North Edisto and Combahee Rivers to harass Confederate positions. *Dai Ching* sailed far up the Combahee escorted by the steamer tug *Clover*. When within a mile of Tar Bluff, it was caught by surprise when a battery of Confederate guns opened fire. *Dai Ching*'s captain immediately gave orders that would have placed the ship in a better position to exchange fire. However, moments later, he realized the pilot had deserted his post at the helm, leaving the ship vulnerable to the winds and an ebb tide. Before the situation could be remedied, *Dai Ching* grounded hard.

Clover attempted to pull *Dai Ching* away, but the hawser broke. Instead of making another attempt to free *Dai Ching*, *Clover* simply sailed away.

For a period of about seven hours, the Confederate guns, said to be a pair of seven-inch Brooks rifles and a smoothbore, played havoc on *Dai Ching*, hitting it over thirty times. The ship was savaged by the hits, and its one hundred pounder was taken out of commission by a direct hit, leaving it without a gun to return fire. A boat with five men was sent downstream to gather assistance from other vessels several miles away but was captured by Confederate pickets.

Dai Ching's crew abandoned ship and huddled in the marsh close to the hull for several hours. Finally realizing help was not coming, they then set the ship afire. With just one small boat available, most of the crew was forced to trudge over four miles through the marsh carrying several wounded sailors before rescue.

Union naval officers were aghast at the circumstances leading to the loss of *Dai Ching*. A major investigation leading to a court-martial was quickly conducted. The civilian pilot, "a colored man who fled below into the fire room" after the first shot, was specifically named for possible punishment, as were two officers of the *Clover*. What actual punishment they might have received is not found, but such gross dereliction of duty and obvious cowardice were charges that could not easily be excused or lightly punished.

In addition to those captured, the *Dai Ching* reported nine men wounded. It was later found that *Dai Ching* had burned to the waterline. No Confederate report on this action is found, and the unit manning the battery involved remains unidentified. Certainly, the men in gray performed well.[34]

A YANKEE GENERAL'S NOT SO NEW IDEA

The War for Southern Independence brought about development of several forms of innovative vessels of war on both sides. Confederate innovations were ironclads, spar-torpedo boats and the submarine *H.L. Hunley*. The major Union contribution to this list was the *Monitor*-class warship. Almost certainly the most far-fetched concept for a vessel from either side in the entire war was designed by Union major general John G. Foster, commanding officer of Union troops around Charleston in 1864. Instead of a modern invention, however, he simply reached back into ancient history.

In August 1864, Foster reported to the U.S. War Department that he was building two similar craft at naval facilities in Beaufort. Calling them "assaulting arks," he described them in some detail:

These will be simply modern row galleys, fifty oars on a side; will draw 26 inches of water when loaded with 1,000 men; will have elevated towers for sharpshooters, and an assaulting ladder or gangplank of 51 feet in length, operated by machinery. These will be useful anywhere, in assaulting a fort or landing troops in shoal water.

The sides of each craft were to have iron plating for protection against musket fire. No mention is found of the precise configuration, length or beam for the craft, but by any stretch of imagination, these galleys would have been massive to adequately accommodate so many fully equipped troops in a single-decked craft. One visualization is that the craft would have fifty files of eighteen men standing shoulder-to-shoulder between the seated rowers, thus requiring a minimum beam of about seventy feet. Allowing for full packs carried by the troops, the assault ladder and its machinery along with the sharpshooters' towers, the length would likely have been two hundred feet or more. Its bow would probably have been sleek to allow the rower's efforts to be most effective. Unfortunately, the schematics drawn by his engineers are not available.

Foster received scant attention or support for this project from his superiors. With Grant's siege of Petersburg and Sherman's campaign in Georgia taking place at this time, all resources were dedicated to their needs, and projects like these were low priorities. Foster's requests for steel plates and other required items were apparently simply ignored by the Quartermaster-General's Office and elsewhere, leaving the project to wither on the vine.[35]

6

SOLDIERS' STORIES

COLONEL JOHN BRATTON AS A PRISONER OF WAR

John Bratton, a native of Winnsboro, South Carolina, served faithfully and creditably during the war. An 1850 graduate of South Carolina College (now the University), he rose on merit from private to brigadier general in 1864. As colonel of his Sixth South Carolina Infantry regiment, on May 31, 1862, he led his men into the Battle of Seven Pines. It would be a day he would remember for the rest of his life.

His regiment, at the forefront of the attacking division, advanced nearly two miles routing numerically larger Union forces, captured two Union camps and crashed through four lines of prepared defensive works before being forced to withdraw. During the withdrawal, he was severely wounded and captured. What followed next is one of the most outstanding displays of chivalry, honor and respect for a foe in the annals of the war.

Passing in and out of consciousness during his withdrawal, Bratton was helped by two of his men and a captured Union captain toward Confederate lines. In the darkness, the small group became separated, leaving him and the captain alone. A short while later, an advancing party of Union soldiers arrived and, on finding Bratton alive, set about to take him to a nearby field hospital. Bratton heard the Union captain tell them, "Handle him gently, boys. He was kind to me."[36]

Despite sensing Bratton's wound was mortal, surgeons at the field hospital provided full treatment. The next morning, Bratton was transferred to a hospital farther in the rear of Union lines. By then, Union commanders were well aware of the events from the day before, and the Sixth South Carolina was mentioned prominently in Northern newspapers and Union reports. When it was learned that the colonel of that regiment had been wounded and captured, Bratton became an instant celebrity. Union general Philip Kearney, commanding the troops capturing Bratton, sent a message to the hospital asking that Bratton "receive the utmost care."

After Bratton's transfer to the hospital at Fort Monroe several weeks later, Kearney sent the prison commander a letter requesting "every consideration should be shown" to Bratton, who was soon moved to a more comfortable cell. At the same time, Kearney sent a letter directly to Bratton. In it, he stated,

I take the liberty, in courtesy and good feeling, of putting myself, or friends of the North, at your disposal. I forward by special messenger your sword, belt and watch, together with a letter from the surgeon...who attended you, who is an acquaintance of your family....I also place at your call credit with my banker...$200.00, which may serve until your own arrangements are made.

Bratton was astounded at such consideration and generosity by a man he had not met. Unfortunately, he never had the opportunity to learn why. General Kearney was killed in the September 1862 Battle of Chantilly one day after Bratton's release. Kearney's death was mourned by many Confederate officers who knew him from prewar days as a gallant warrior and as a gentleman. Perhaps Kearney recognized and wished to acknowledge the profound warrior traits displayed in Bratton's leadership at Seven Pines. Kearney's letter was kept by Bratton as a treasured memento until his death in 1898.[37]

PRIVATE JOSEPH HARRISON AND HIS MOMENT OF COURAGE

Confederate privates were rarely mentioned in the after-action reports of their senior commanders. Countless deeds of courage were known but never documented and became lost over time. Private Joseph Harrison, Company G, First (Butler's) South Carolina Infantry, was an exception.

Harrison enlisted in January 1862 in Savannah. His regiment, trained as both infantry and artillery, spent most of the war at Fort Moultrie and elsewhere around Charleston. Their first taste of battle came on April 7, 1863, when nine Union monitors and ironclads attacked Fort Moultrie. The resulting two-hour-long action, termed the First Battle of Charleston Harbor, resulted in a humiliating defeat of the Union flotilla and brought Private Harrison to the attention of many.

As the Union warships neared Fort Moultrie that day, gun crews there began placing their guns in position to meet them. Harrison, working to get his assigned gun ready, had something go terribly wrong. While details are not given, the results were that the little finger on his left hand was accidentally cut off and he was taken away quickly for treatment. Shortly afterward, certainly to the surprise of his compatriots in arms, he returned to his station to carry out his duties throughout the engagement.

Harrison's determination to serve in time of battle despite his injury was an inspiration to those on his gun and, indeed, the rest of the fort. His deed is recorded in after-action reports from his regimental and brigade commanders. Each gave him praise, and one rightfully described his deed as "Heroic Conduc.t" There can be little doubt of the high esteem in which he was held by his fellow soldiers. Unfortunately, the injury sidelined him for several weeks, keeping him "Absent, sick in quarters."

On October 1, 1863, he was promoted to corporal and shortly afterward detailed for several weeks with the Quartermaster Department. On May 12, 1864, Private Harrison was placed on detached service as a boat hand at Fort Moultrie. This change in status caused him to lose his corporal stripes and revert to private. He served in this capacity until Charleston was evacuated in February 1865.

Upon evacuation of Charleston, Harrison was reunited with his regiment, which was placed in a brigade under the command of Colonel Alfred Rhett. It joined with other Confederate units in front of the Union army advancing through the Palmetto State under Union general W.T. Sherman. Harrison and his regiment fought with distinction in the thirteen-hour-long engagement at Averasboro, North Carolina, and then again in the three-day Battle of Bentonville. He was among those who received parole at Greensboro, North Carolina, when the Confederate army surrendered to Sherman.

Despite intense research efforts, Joseph Harrison's prewar and postwar years remain mysteries. All that is known of the life of this brave, determined and loyal soldier comes from his service record. Though wherever he came from and whatever he did after the war are unknown, his moment of courage at Fort Moultrie was recorded and made available for posterity.[38]

WADE HAMPTON'S IRON SCOUTS: CONFEDERATE SPECIAL FORCES

Hampton's Iron Scouts wartime activities were lost to historians until very recently, when their extraordinary service was finally recovered. Known officially during the war simply as Hampton's Scouts, their service was unique in that it was nearly entirely from within the enemy lines.

Wade Hampton's Iron Scouts were a key part of J.E.B. Stuart's widespread and highly effective intelligence network for the Army of Northern Virginia. Serving with distinction from December 1862 until the war's end in April 1865, they can legitimately be described as a Confederate Special Forces unit because of their unique roles and missions. Formed in secrecy, the Scouts operated in secrecy, and when the war ended, their story remained hidden until 2018, when the first in-depth study of their service was released in book form.

Hampton's Scouts were born of necessity. Union general Ambrose Burnside's move on Fredericksburg in November 1862 went undetected for nearly three full days, and Confederate general Robert E. Lee learned of it not through his army but from civilians in Burnside's path. Though Lee rebounded nicely from this shocking news and ultimately defeated Burnside at Fredericksburg, he realized how vulnerable he had been and sought ways to prevent being surprised again. Shortly after the battle, he and his high command devised a novel plan that was way ahead of its time. It called for scouts to be stationed behind enemy lines on a permanent presence basis for the purposes of detecting and reporting enemy threats.

With the plan handed off to Wade Hampton to implement, Hampton and his men devised an operational unit that can be described as energetic and aggressive in every way. It is thought they relied on the legacy of South Carolina's Francis Marion, the "Swamp Fox," for its basis. One hundred years later, the U.S. military in Vietnam unknowingly replicated much of what Hampton's Scouts did in the 1860s through the use of Marine Recon Teams, Army Long Range Reconnaissance Patrols (LRRPs) and the Green Berets.

Hampton initially formed the platoon-sized detachment from his Deep South cavalry, mostly with South Carolinians from his old Hampton Legion Cavalry Battalion. Men were taken from other commands as the war continued. Though the Scouts averaged about twenty men on their roster at any one time, just seventy-two men are known to have ridden in the unit in its twenty-eight-month existence. While small in numbers, their value to the Army of Northern Virginia and their effect on the war in Virginia were enormous. Over fifty of the Scouts had South Carolina ties. The others were from North Carolina, Alabama, Mississippi and Georgia.

They were all enlisted men—privates, corporals and sergeants—with a sergeant commanding them, and each was appointed by his regimental commander. One source wrote, "When a man was appointed as a Scout, it meant he was cool and courageous at all times. No ordinary man could fill the position."[39]

When a Scout left Confederate lines, he was not expected to return unless carrying a report or bringing in prisoners. Each man carried two or more revolvers, and if he had a shoulder weapon, it was usually a double-barrel shotgun. A Scout was responsible for providing his own nourishment and forage for his horse. He expected to sleep in the forest, in fields, in abandoned buildings and, occasionally, at homes of friendly Virginians. He carried food with him and supplemented it at times from the haversacks and saddlebags of captured Yankees and, occasionally, a home-cooked meal from friendly Virginia families. Scouts received no extra pay, no promotions, no special privileges—no tangible reward of any sort.

Four of the Scouts' distinct missions mirror those of today's Special Forces. First, foremost and always was the gathering of military intelligence. They didn't scout as a team of twenty but were split into multiple teams with the sizes depending on the mission and the territory to be covered. Usually, teams were two to six men but never less than a pair. They often had to ride close to their target, dismount and travel several miles by foot before they could lay eyes on the enemy position. They watched the railroad, base camps and supply depots while monitoring troop movements and observing camp activities. They looked for signs of impending moves such as sudden troop movements or concentrations, the cooking of extra rations and distribution of ammunition, the loading and forming of wagon trains and so on. In 1864, they were along the James River, monitoring Union shipping and watching what came in and what went out. Their timely, accurate and detailed reports gave their generals—Lee, Stuart and Hampton—an in-depth view, wide and deep, of enemy activities, positions and strength. The Scouts detected enemy movements prior to the Mine Run Campaign, the Dahlgren-Kilpatrick Raid, Grant's Overland Campaign and the Battles of Trevilian Station and Second Deep Bottom. Additionally, they gave early warning of every single one of Grant's moves below Petersburg in 1864. This was dangerous work, and one source wrote, "On an average day, a good scout rode with information in one hand and his life in the other."[40]

Wade Hampton summed up the work of his Scouts in a succinct yet highly informative statement:

> *Living constantly within the lines of the enemy, no movement escaped their observations & I was kept regularly appraised not only of the position, but of the strength, organization, & often even of the very purposes of the enemy.*[41]

This profound statement clearly demonstrates the value of the reports the Scouts sent in. It also demonstrates that Lee, Stuart and Hampton usually had sufficient information at critical times to make reasoned and deliberate decisions before committing troops to meet Yankee threats. One source wrote,

> *It is hard to place the proper estimate upon the great work that the Scouts accomplished for the Confederate government. They kept General Lee better posted as to the movements of the Yankee army than a great many of the Union generals knew themselves.*[42]

The second mission is termed *unconventional warfare* by today's Special Forces but simply refers to conducting guerrilla warfare. The Scouts had an immediate and powerful effect and created nightmares for the enemy with their guerrilla activities within Union lines. Small Union patrols, reserve picket posts and couriers were gobbled up by the Scouts. In the span of just a couple of months, their guerrilla activities led to decrees by Union generals that cavalry patrols should consist of no fewer than fifty men! These decrees lasted until the end of the war.

The third mission carried out by the Scouts is termed *direct action* by today's Special Forces. This means the unit transitioned into a strike force when circumstances allowed for it. The sergeant commanding the Scouts regularly called in his teams to form a strike force when the opportunity arose to ambush vulnerable large Union cavalry patrols. In February 1863

Sergeant J. Dickerson "Dick" Hogan of the Second South Carolina Cavalry and a principal member of Wade Hampton's Iron Scouts. *From* Butler and His Cavalry in the War of Secession, 1861–1865.

alone, a sixty-four-man company of Union cavalry was destroyed by just eleven Scouts and a forty-five-man cavalry company was annihilated by seventeen Scouts. The crowning moment, however, was when fifteen Scouts ambushed and utterly routed an enemy cavalry regiment.[43]

The fourth mission was to find and identify targets of opportunity too large for them to handle. Present-day Special Forces, on finding such targets, can call in artillery fire, air support or, at times, naval gunfire to cause its destruction. Hampton's Scouts did not have these assets but were still able to achieve the same results. They would send one of their men to General Hampton or his subordinates advising that they had the opportunity to hit an enemy position or vulnerable Union unit too large for them to take on. However, if they were granted forty or fifty well-armed men to give the necessary firepower, the task could be completed. Invariably, their requests were granted and the Scouts were able to follow through with their plan. The most notable target of opportunity mission achieved was Hampton's famous Great Beefsteak Raid in September 1864. The Scouts detected Grant's 2,500 head of cattle near his City Point headquarters and advised Hampton the cattle were vulnerable and actually presented a plan for taking the herd. Hampton used their plan and other information they provided as the basis for the raid and gave them much credit for its success.

The Scouts had two other occasional missions that would not be applicable to today's Special Forces. One of them was carrying communications between the Confederate high command and Confederate agents far behind the Union lines as far north as Alexandria, Virginia. This shows the full and complete trust given them from the highest levels. The other mission was Hampton's use of the Scouts on a tactical basis. Whenever going into battle, Hampton carried some of his Scouts with him to monitor the enemy movements and their flanks. At least one instance is known where Hampton hit a weak spot discovered by his Scouts and broke the Union line.

The Scouts wore Confederate uniforms in all phases of the war. During the winters, some wore captured Union greatcoats for warmth and, at times, used them for deception. Had a Scout been captured in a complete Union uniform, he would have been liable for execution as a spy. Twenty-nine Scouts were captured during the war, and not a single one faced this dilemma.

Hampton's Scouts were given the nickname "Iron Scouts" by their Union foe, almost certainly in early 1863, because they seemed to be bulletproof. Numerous accounts exist to attest why this name was deemed so fitting up to the war's end. Though others were wounded, just four were killed in performance of their scouting duties.

No other scouting unit in either army served as long as Hampton's Iron Scouts, nor did any serve with the same variety of missions. Unquestionably, they had the most dangerous job in the army, and when they spoke, the generals—Hampton, Stuart and Lee—listened.[44]

The Most Heavily Shelled Men in the War

The most intensely bombarded site in the War for Southern Independence was Fort Sumter. Guarding Charleston's harbor, it endured three major bombardments and eight minor ones from Union guns on Morris Island and the Union fleet close ashore between August 17, 1863, and the fall of Charleston in February 1865. Those bombardments, plus additional regular desultory fire, totaled approximately forty-seven thousand heavy shells from rifled guns and mortars with an estimated weight of 3,500 tons.

Major Stephen Elliott, a Beaufort native and commander of the fort from early September 1863 until early May 1864, became the most heavily shelled soldier of either side. In his eight months of command, Fort Sumter was targeted by Union guns over twenty-one thousand times. His solid and unruffled performance during the forty-one-day Second Great Bombardment, in which nearly nineteen thousand shells were hurled at the fort, earned him promotion to lieutenant colonel through executive order of President Jefferson Davis.

Unmentioned in most history books is another South Carolinian, William Richard Cathcart (1843–1898). Cathcart, son of an Irish immigrant, lived in Columbia with his family when war erupted. Nothing is known of his work or training until we find him reporting to Fort Sumter as a civilian telegrapher in August 1863 at age nineteen. He certainly would have not been assigned to that vital post without proven experience and ability.

Unfortunately for Cathcart, his arrival coincided with the First Great Bombardment of Sumter. Lasting from August 17 to September 2, it saw nearly seven thousand shells fired at Sumter from Union guns on Morris Island and Yankee ships. This prolonged shelling put the fort in near-total ruins and destroyed it as an artillery bastion. Never again would Fort Sumter fire a gun against the enemy.

Elliott took command of Fort Sumter shortly afterward. From that point on, he and Cathcart endured the various periods of shelling until May 1864. These two men were the only ones at Sumter not relieved or rotated during this period. Cathcart's performance under Elliott was highly credible, dependable and efficient even in the most difficult times. Their work brought them into regular contact on a daily basis and apparently developed into friendship and a deep respect for each other.

A major fire at Sumter on December 12, 1863, destroyed Cathcart's spare clothing and personal articles, but Elliott's request to have the army replace these items was denied because of Cathcart's civilian status. Still, Cathcart remained on duty at Fort Sumter and did not leave until Elliott was transferred in May 1864. Both Elliott and Cathcart received much-deserved recognition on leaving the fort. Elliott's splendid performance earned him promotion to colonel. Cathcart's service at Sumter must have also been viewed as exceptional and meritorious, for he became "Superintendent [of] Military Telegraph Lines" despite his youthful age of twenty.

After the war, Cathcart returned to Columbia, where he spent most of his later life as manager of the Western Union Telegraph office. While Elliott was lucky to have been wounded just once by over twenty-one thousand shells fired at Sumter in his eight months of service there, Cathcart somehow avoiding being hit by any of over twenty-eight thousand during his nine-month tenure. Cathcart emerged by far the most heavily shelled individual of the war and, perhaps, the luckiest. That each man retained his sanity, composure and ability to function normally despite such shelling shows intestinal fortitude and unwavering devotion to duty found in few.[45]

CAPTAIN WAMPLER, A VIRGINIAN IN CHARLESTON

There is a personal story for each of the hundreds of Confederate servicemen buried in Soldiers Ground at Magnolia Cemetery in Charleston. That of Captain J. Morris Wampler, a Virginian, is powerful and compelling. When war erupted, Wampler enlisted in the Eighth Virginia Infantry, but in February 1862 he was appointed captain in the Corps of Engineers. His skills and energy led him to be named chief engineer of the Army of Tennessee. However, in June 1863 while with the Army of Tennessee in Chattanooga, he requested transfer to the Army of Northern Virginia with a poignant letter reading in part:

> *It is now more than two years since I left my family & home in Loudon Co., Virginia. Since then, the enemy have devastated my home, destroyed or stolen everything, abused my wife, mother & my five little helpless children. Whenever I hear of an advance of our forces toward the Potomac, I feel that this is no place for me, I should be where I naturally belong, in the* [Army of Northern Virginia.] *I might then have occasional opportunities of aiding my family and of doing my share toward driving the enemy from my home.*

While his transfer request was pending, Captain Wampler was sent to Charleston and named chief engineer at Battery Wagner on Morris Island. Arriving in early July 1863, he provided distinguished service and was cited for his efficiency and personal courage during the intense actions and bombardments that followed. Sadly, he was killed in mid-August when hit by shrapnel from a shell fired by a Union monitor.

Captain Wampler was mourned but not forgotten. An earthwork with several cannon emplacements later erected near Fort Johnson was named Battery Wampler in his honor. Though no traces of the site remain, the road leading to it remains in use today and is aptly named Wampler Drive. This displaced Virginian who never wavered in his duties despite his personal worries lies at rest at Soldiers Ground among other brave and dedicated men whose stories are yet to be told.[46]

The Incredible Captain Joseph B. Lyle

Captain Joseph Banks Lyle, born in Fairfield County in 1829, was a graduate of South Carolina College and an educator. He was master of a boy's school in York when war erupted, and he longed for the day he could return to his chosen profession.

October 27, 1864, promised to be another day of battle for Lyle, a member of the Fifth South Carolina Infantry. A seasoned soldier with service dating to April 13, 1861, he was in command of skirmishers for Bratton's Brigade in Field's Division. The expected battle that day found the Confederate forces along a portion of Richmond's outer defensive line grossly outnumbered by Union forces poised to their front. It marked the first action under Lieutenant General James Longstreet since his recovery from wounds received at The Wilderness several months earlier. After a series of Union feints, Longstreet's battle instincts led him to believe the real threat was at undefended works farther down the lines a couple of miles at Williamsburg Road. Confederate cavalry had engaged and routed a much larger Union cavalry command there that morning but was no longer in the area to protect it. Accordingly, he took a calculated risk and dispatched Field's division to occupy the position.

Longstreet's hunch proved prophetic, for no sooner had Field's men

Captain Joseph Banks Lyle, credited with the capture of between five and six hundred Union soldiers virtually single-handedly at the Battle of Williamsburg Road in October 1864. *Author's collection.*

occupied the works than a Union assault commenced. The Yankees believed the position to be undefended and advanced unhurriedly from their starting point about a mile away. The attackers were caught in the open and totally shocked when Field's men opened fire on them. Those not hit either fled the scene or took shelter in a number of nearby gullies. Seeing no chance of success for continuing the attack, their only thoughts centered on escaping their predicament. The Yankees soon realized the gullies led back to their starting point and began dashing from one gulley to another in hope of escaping the killing field under covering fire of their artillery and approaching darkness.

Lyle, sensing the enemy was beaten, demoralized and desiring only to escape, felt they would surrender if he was allowed to take his skirmishers forward. His request to do so was denied, and many more Union soldiers escaped. Lyle did not want to have to fight these Yankees again on another day when he felt they could be so easily captured. Then, unwilling to see such an opportunity pass and on his own volition, he stepped beyond Confederate lines to demand their surrender. Confederate forces on each end of the lines, thinking Lyle was a deserter, opened fire on him. However, word quickly spread that this was not the case and the firing was quickly ceased.

On reaching the main part of the remaining Union force well over one hundred yards away, Lyle audaciously demanded their surrender and instructed the forlorn Yankees to march toward the Confederate line—and they began doing so! Apparently, Lyle was blessed with what is known as command presence. As a seasoned schoolmaster and hardened Confederate captain, his verbal orders likely carried the voice of authority.

After about half had filed away, a Union officer challenged him by urging his men not to surrender to a single Confederate soldier but to pick up their arms and fight. Lyle reacted quickly by picking up a carbine discarded in the earlier cavalry engagement, advanced on the officer and threatened to kill him if he did not surrender at once. The threat worked, and the officer joined those marching to Confederate lines.

Lyle wrote in his diary that he captured at least four hundred Yankees before the skirmishers finally were sent to support him. Afterward, he was credited with single-handedly capturing between five and six hundred prisoners plus several stands of colors and swords. That night, when all was quiet, Lyle learned the carbine he had used was empty. Generals Longstreet, Field and Bratton each cited him for this outstanding display of personal courage and accomplishment. The Confederate War Department promoted him to major in March 1865, but the fall of Richmond prevented the commission from reaching him.[47]

Somehow, this incredible feat languished in obscurity until it was rediscovered in 1996. The Sons of Confederate Veterans honored him in 2003 with a Confederate Medal of Honor. Lyle's deed is unique in that he neither fired a shot nor had close support, a far different situation than Sergeant York of World War I fame. York received the Medal of Honor for leading a squad of sixteen men into German lines and killing 25 German soldiers while capturing 130.

The Battle of Williamsburg Road stopped what was likely the most dangerous threat to Richmond during the entire war, and had the Union plan worked, the city would have been wide open for the taking months before it finally was captured. This battle, like Lyle, is rarely addressed. Longstreet's battlefield instincts saved the day, but Lyle's action put the exclamation point on it.

SERVICE IN THE CONFEDERATE SIGNAL CORPS AT CHARLESTON

Service in the Signal Corps has rarely been addressed by historians. The corps formed in April 1862, and fewer than 1,600 men served in its ranks. Though most of its records are lost, sufficient documentation is available to reveal a clear insight to its composition and nature of service.

The corps in Charleston was composed almost entirely of enlisted men detached from various infantry, artillery and cavalry commands. Each could be returned to his unit when no longer needed or when recalled by his parent command. The men, all privates, were energetic and bright. Taught to send signals by flags in the day and by lights and torches at night, these signal operators worked in teams of three or four men at stations all around Charleston. Additionally, two men were usually assigned to each of the ironclad gunboats in the harbor.

In July 1863, then-signals officer Lieutenant Frank Markoe reported that of the forty-six men on his roster, six were temporarily serving in another district and five others were sick and unable to resume field duty for some time. He added that the bare minimum to operate adequately with was thirty-eight men. It is apparent that while the corps was essential, it was quite small.

The Signal Corps offered no room for promotions but did allow a limited number of men to be designated "lance sergeant," a temporary rank allowing a private to act as a sergeant but at the pay of a private. The few given this rank earned it by demonstrating leadership, proficiency and courage at the highest levels. Members of the corps, whatever their rank, had access to senior officers at all times. Enduring the same hardships and dangers as everyone else in their various stations, the men of the Signal Corps were recognized for their courage as well as their work and routinely given the same respect a commissioned officer might receive.

Each month, hundreds of signals around Charleston were sent and received. Handling such volumes required the signal posts to be alert at all hours of the day regardless of weather or hazards such as enemy shelling. Team members worked closely together to allow for proper rest, meals and other needs. Two men were required to send or receive a message. When receiving, one would call out the observed signals while the other wrote them down. When sending, one signaled while the other called out the appropriate signal to send. High-volume stations required frequent rotation to keep teams from becoming exhausted. All in all, their work was demanding and vital, and these signals operators overcame many hardships, challenges and dangers in carrying out their tasks.

They were instrumental in another way. In April 1863, they cracked the signal code being used by Union commanders around Charleston and began a close monitor on those communications. Union messages were read regularly until September 1863, when a new cipher was put in use. Confederate commanders feared that the Yankees had learned that the previous code had been broken but were relieved when the old code was reinstated a short while later. From that point on, most Union messages were read until Charleston was evacuated in February 1865. Commanders of Forts Sumter, Moultrie and Johnson, as well as Batteries Wagner and Gregg, were often forewarned when targeted for direct assault or close bombardment from Union ships. Given time to prepare their positions against these threats, the posts were able to meet and frustrate well-laid plans by Union commanders.

Signal operators were expected to send and receive messages during the foulest of weather conditions. They were also expected to perform in the heat of battle. Numerous records attest that the operators carried out their roles during the heaviest of actions at Battery Wagner, Fort Sumter and elsewhere. Disregarding bullets and exploding shells, the men stood in exposed positions to send their vital messages and receive others. From mid-July through mid-September 1863, at least a dozen members, nearly one-third of the Signal Corps in Charleston, were wounded.

At Battery Gregg on Morris Island, where their service was especially crucial and equally dangerous, Signal Corps members were cited several times for heroism and efficiency amid the worst of the fighting. Five of the Corps, each a South Carolinian, were named to the Confederate Roll of Honor maintained by the Confederate War Department in Richmond in acknowledgement of their performance at that position. One of them, Lance Sergeant F.K. Huger, was again cited for leadership and heroism during the Union small boat attack on Fort Sumter on September 9, 1863.

Placed in charge of a detachment armed with hand grenades and fire-balls, he and his men performed flawlessly in the engagement. The citation from Sumter's commander, Major Stephen Elliott, reads:

> *I have the honor to bring to the notice of the Department, the distinguished services of Sergt. F.K. Huger of the Signal Corps during the assault on this post on the 9th inst. Acting as my assistant, his clearness of judgements, facility of command and rapidity of execution, contributed in a marked degree to the success of the affair. I respectfully recommend that steps be taken to secure him a commission.*[48]

The Signal Corps in Charleston enjoyed a fine reputation. Though its members may never have fired a gun, their contributions to the defense of Charleston warrant the highest respect.[49]

PRIVATE JOSEPH P. HUGER: HE JUST WANTED TO BE A SOLDIER

Confederate history is full of stories about young men and their service in the army. That of Charlestonian Joseph P. Huger (1846–1864) is among those full of hope and admiration but with a tragic ending. Though barely a minor footnote in the overall study of the war, it brings to light a young man's patriotism and desire to serve his new nation when he was under no obligation to do so.

On December 22, 1863, seventeen-year-old Huger wrote a letter to General P.G.T. Beauregard's chief of staff, General Thomas Jordan. The letter read, "I have the honor to request an appointment to the Signal Corps as the state of my health prevents me from joining any other branch of the army." No information specifying his health problem is found.

The Signal Corps had no way of directly enlisting a man and depended exclusively on qualified volunteers from other branches of the service being detached, subject to recall, by their regiments. Accordingly, Huger was advised by Lieutenant Frank Markoe, Charleston's signals officer, that he must be lawfully enlisted in an army command and then ask to be detached to the Signal Corps.

It appears Huger met with Lieutenant Markoe over the next few weeks and that Markoe was satisfied Huger's intelligence, attitude and physical condition were sufficient for performance of Signal Corps duties. On January 21, 1864, Huger enlisted in Company A Manigault's Battalion of South Carolina Artillery, in Charleston. Arrangements almost certainly were in place for him to be detached to the Signal Corps, for the transfer request was submitted and approved the next day. He was officially detached on January 23 in what is likely a record for army efficiency.

Huger's service record shows nothing of his training, but he had to learn to send and receive signals at all hours. In daytime, they would be sent via signal flags and at night via lighted torches. Huger must have become proficient quickly and satisfied Lieutenant Markoe and those training him. His natural talents and positive attitude seemingly outweighed any health issues he had and likely endeared him to Markoe and others working with him. His military service records indicate he was soon assigned as part of the Signal Corps team at Fort Sumter, a most important site requiring skilled and efficient signal operators.[50]

On April 13, 1864, Lieutenant Colonel Stephen Elliott, commanding Fort Sumter, sent several messages. One of those was a request to Beauregard asking permission to fire a thirteen-gun salute at noon in honor of the capture of Fort Sumter on that date in 1861. The request was quickly approved, and plans were set in place to proceed. Shortly afterward, Elliott sent his final message that day, advising Beauregard that "J.P. Huger, Signal Corps, was killed half an hour ago by a Parrott Shell."

The Yankees fired twenty-three shells at Sumter that day, and Huger was the only casualty. He was part of the three-man team on duty and exposed on the fort's rampart when hit. Though numerous Signals Corps operators around Charleston were wounded through the war, his was the only death.

Private Joseph P. Huger's military service lasted less than three months, and his death came six months prior to his eighteenth birthday. Huger's family buried him in Charleston's magnificent Magnolia Cemetery with his story known only to precious few since.

SOUTH CAROLINA'S BOY COLONEL: JAMES R. HAGOOD

The Confederate army was filled with many young men in their teens who served with ranks from private up to captain. A South Carolinian, James R. Hagood, younger brother of well-known General Johnson Hagood, went even further by earning promotion to colonel of his regiment at age eighteen.

James Hagood left The Military Academy of South Carolina (The Citadel) as a sophomore; enlisted as a private in the First (Hagood's) South Carolina Infantry Regiment on July 1, 1862; and was elected the regimental sergeant major at age seventeen. He seems to have been marked for destiny, for, before the year's end, he was elected second lieutenant and then captain as well as serving at one point as regimental adjutant. Additionally, in this period he led his company action in several battles involving the Army of Northern Virginia, including Second Manassas and Sharpsburg. Despite his youthful age, he soon was tasked with serving on examining committees and courts-martial, positions attesting to his military knowledge, reputation and standing.

His regiment went with Longstreet to Georgia and Tennessee in late 1863. While there, his brigade commander Brigadier General Micah Jenkins recommended Hagood for promotion from captain to colonel of his regiment based on Hagood's "Valor and Skill." Bypassing the ranks of major and lieutenant colonel was almost unheard of in promotion to colonel, but Jenkins apparently felt the exceptions in this instance were appropriate. The War Department confirmed this promotion on November 16, 1863, just two days before Hagood's nineteenth birthday, making him the youngest colonel in the Confederate army.

Hagood was fortunate to serve in the superb Jenkins (later Bratton's) Brigade in Field's Division of Longstreet's Corps with top-notch leadership at each level. He led his regiment in many of the major engagements of the Army of Northern Virginia in 1864, including The Wilderness, Spotsylvania Court House, Cold Harbor and the Petersburg siege. He was paroled at Appomattox Court House in April 1865 at age twenty. His record as a regimental commander stands strong and unblemished.

In 1868, General Robert E. Lee wrote about young Hagood: "During the whole time of his connection to the Army of Northern Virginia he was conspicuous for his gallantry, good conduct and efficiency. By his merit constantly exhibited, he rose from a private in his regiment to its command, and showed by his actions he was worthy of the position." Major General Charles Field, his division commander, wrote, "Colonel Hagood's high-toned, soldierly bearing at all times, his thorough handling of his regiment, and his distinguished gallantry in action, won my admiration and regard." Such praise validates Hagood's meteor-like rise through the ranks while he was still in his teens. It confirms that those above him saw the same fine leadership qualities as those with whom he served and led.[51]

James Hagood, having survived the horrors of war without being wounded, lost his life in a tragic train accident in 1870 at age twenty-six. He left behind a legacy of excellence as a man, a soldier and a leader. He is buried in Barnwell County, South Carolina, the site of his birth.

DEFIANCE AT FORT SUMTER

Numerous battles and skirmishes occurred along coastal South Carolina from Beaufort to Little River, and the annals contain many accounts of the heroism and valor performed by Confederate soldiers. Charleston, the epicenter of the war in the state, saw valor in every form, especially with the Battle of Battery Wagner in the summer of 1863.

Fort Sumter was different from any other engagement in that its men could not return fire and fight back. From mid-August 1863 until mid-February 1865, when Charleston was evacuated, the fort had not a single gun available to return enemy fire. The garrison, pummeled by heavy shells from the Union fleet and guns on Morris Island, could do little more than hunker down while remaining alert for an assault by Yankee landing parties. Yet even in this one-sided situation, numerous accounts of heroism by Sumter's defenders in small groups or as individuals are etched in the records. Two of these accounts are so conspicuous and brazen that Hollywood movie directors would likely not depict them because their audiences would not believe they could have actually occurred.

The first event happened late on October 31, 1863, the sixth day of the forty-one-day Second Major Bombardment of Sumter. Union guns fired 1,005 shells at Sumter that day, killing fifteen and wounding four others. It was a terrible day for the garrison, part of which was the Twelfth Georgia Light Artillery Battalion, which was serving as infantry. Twice the men of that command went to great lengths in replacing the fort's flag after it was shot down, and the men performing these acts were cited by the fort's commander in his daily report. Yet there was to be one more feat to follow.

Just before sundown, despite shells exploding on and over the fort, the battalion's band assembled and went to the parapet, facing the enemy on nearby Cummings Point. There, they "played 'The Bonnie Blue Flag' with as much spirit as if on dress parade. The firing from Cummings Point [on Morris Island] immediately ceased and a [Union] band marched to the sea beach and answered with 'The Star-Spangled Banner.' The cheers of the sailors on Union monitors and from the Federal garrison on Morris Island were distinctly heard on Fort Sumter despite the roar of artillery [elsewhere]." No mention is made that the bands played other songs, but for at least a brief interval, the shelling was stopped.[52]

The other remarkable event took place on January 30, 1864, amid the Third Minor Bombardment of Fort Sumter. The action is described by Lieutenant Colonel Stephen Elliott in his daily report: "At 3:00 PM the flag staff was shot down; it was first replaced upon a small and afterwards upon a larger staff by Private F. Schafer of Company A, Lucas's Battalion, who stood upon the top of the traverse and repeatedly waved the flag in the sight of the enemy."

After Schafer placed the flag staff on the fort's wall, a Union shell landed nearby, narrowly missing him and the flag. Elliott continued his report: "At the close of the scene, Schafer, springing from a cloud of the smoke and dust of the bursting shell, stood long waving his hat in triumph. It was a most gallant deed, and the effect upon the garrison was most inspiring."[53]

Neither feat was planned. Each was a heat-of-the moment reaction of audacious defiance by enlisted men serving in the most severe and desperate situation imaginable. Their actions sent a clear message that the incessant shelling would not drive them from their post at Fort Sumter, something for which the Union forces had no answer.

THE GALLANT PRIVATE WILLIAM A. BOLICK

William A. Bolick of Chester, South Carolina, first entered Confederate service as a private in the First South Carolina Infantry (Butler's) early in 1861 at age seventeen. Described as being slightly cross-eyed, he easily transformed from a blacksmith's son into a fine and well-respected soldier. In June 1862, after his initial enlistment expired, he joined Company K, First South Carolina Cavalry, and was immediately sent to Virginia. There, he saw much action and quickly distinguished himself as a capable and daring cavalryman.

Bolick was appointed as one of Wade Hampton's "Iron Scouts" in late July 1863 and immediately began building a reputation as a superb addition. Hard riding with numerous combat actions showed his mettle as one who remained cool and collected despite the circumstances. Barely six weeks after becoming a scout, Bolick was one of "a party of 12 select men" chosen personally by General J.E.B. Stuart to raid a Union camp for the purpose of capturing a Yankee general. This daring and dangerous raid failed to make the capture but caused casualties and much embarrassment to the Yankees. It also solidified Bolick's reputation.

The next month, Bolick and another scout infiltrated and surveyed General Meade's headquarters camp well behind Union lines. As they departed, the daring duo captured five Yankees along with their horses and arms without alerting other troops nearby. This bold exploit made Northern newspapers, bringing criticism and additional embarrassment to Meade. The two Scouts received great praise from both Stuart and Robert E. Lee.

Bolick continued his scouting through autumn and into the winter until February 14, 1864. On that day, Bolick and nine other Scouts ambushed a large Union patrol near Brentsville, Virginia. One report stated that seventeen of the twenty-one Yankees were shot. Unfortunately, Bolick was killed in that action. Sensing Union reinforcements were nearby, the other Scouts had little choice but to wrap Bolick's body in a blanket and place it in nearby woods before departing the scene. His loss was acutely painful to his compatriots, and their later actions showed they had no intentions of leaving him unattended. What happened next reflects the closeness within Hampton's Scouts and shows the respect Bolick had from his peers.

Two days after Bolick's death, a team of Scouts returned to the scene with a coffin in a two-horse wagon and recovered his body. They then drove to a site near his Virginia sweetheart's home at Arrington's Crossroads and buried him there. This trip of about ten miles, requiring as much as three hours, was made in broad daylight despite being well within enemy lines and in an area heavily patrolled by Union cavalry. Certainly, there were scouts in front and behind the wagon to warn of any approaching Union patrols. The Iron Scouts, always careful to avoid unnecessary risks, felt that providing a suitable burial for one of their own outweighed the dangers.

Arrington's Crossroads was later renamed David's Crossroads. The area was eventually absorbed by the Quantico Marine Corps base. Diligent searches for his grave have been fruitless. It is presumed Bolick's grave site was somehow forgotten and is lost to posterity. Yet the courage and boldness of this superb soldier who died at age twenty remains and is bequeathed to us as his legacy. His burial, with the story behind it, is one of the most remarkable in the annals of the entire war.[54]

NOTABLE ARTILLERY SHOTS OF THE WAR

Artillery commands from both sides prided themselves on their marksmanship. Numerous accounts exist of phenomenal accuracy. During the siege of Charleston, Union gunners aboard vessels as well as those on Morris Island delighted in hitting the flagstaff at Fort Sumter. Their success was always temporary, as the fort's garrison quickly put another staff in place to bear the fort's flag.

Perhaps the best single shot in the siege was in November 1863 after a shell fired from Morris Island took down Sumter's flagstaff. Members of the fort's garrison promptly prepared another, and as they were in the act of placing it on the parapet, a shell fired from a Union monitor at some distance hit the staff, taking it completely out of their hands. It should be noted that the soldiers involved quickly recovered the flag, affixed it to a new staff and placed it in position to again billow in the ocean breezes atop the rampart.[55]

General James Longstreet wrote about the best two shots he witnessed in combat. One was that of a Union cannon that fired a single shot at General D.H. Hill, mounted and in the open, at a distance of about a mile during the Battle of Sharpsburg. The shell hit Hill's horse, taking off both forelegs. The other superb shot Longstreet mentions is one fired at a Union engineer at Yorktown. The officer walked into the open some distance away carrying a seat and a table, at which he sat and began sketching the Confederate works. A corporal of the Richmond Howitzers took offense at such insolence. Without orders, he turned and aimed his ten-pound Parrott rifle, then fired. His shot dropped directly on the table before exploding, mortally wounding the Yankee.[56]

The deadliest and best-known shot of the entire war was one fired in the Battle of St. Charles on the White River in Arkansas on June 17, 1862. There, a shell from a Confederate thirty-two-pounder penetrated the casemate of the gunboat USS *Mound City* and went through the steam drum of its boiler, filling the vessel's interior with scalding steam. The steam killed 105 men and seriously burned or scalded another 45. The strange part of this well-known story is that the ship was otherwise lightly damaged and managed to be repaired. Still, the number of casualties from this single shot has no comparison.

Perhaps the most results-oriented single shot fired by a Confederate field artillery piece took place near Beaufort on April 9, 1863. There, a Union army gunboat, the *George Washington*, had two shots fired at it from a mile away as it sailed on the Whale Branch River. One missed, but the other hit the ship squarely from astern knocking out its rudder and steering gear, exploding the ammunition magazine and setting the vessel afire. Numerous casualties were incurred, and the crew abandoned ship as it burned to the waterline. It was a spectacular long-range shot for a brass cannon and sweet revenge for Confederate forces in the area. The gunboat had been a thorn in their side for months, and its destruction was celebrated accordingly.[57]

UNRAVELING A HIDDEN STORY

A soldier's Compiled Service Record can provide a wealth of information on a man's service experiences but all too often leaves a researcher with more questions than answers. A prime example of this is found in the service record of Private William B. Morrow of Company G, Second South Carolina Cavalry. Morrow, a native of Greenwood, South Carolina, was mustered into Confederate service at age twenty-five in April 1862. His records show he was wounded and captured at Accotink, Virginia, on July 19, 1863, barely two weeks after the Battle of Gettysburg. This is where multiple questions arise.

A glance at a map shows Accotink to be about seven miles from Alexandria, Virginia, outside of Washington, D.C. Morrow's capture occurred just three days after the Army of Northern Virginia completed its withdrawal from Gettysburg by crossing the Potomac into Virginia. What was Morrow doing in Accotink when his regiment was nearly one hundred miles away? Not a hint is given in his records.

Further, what was happening at Accotink at this time? A search of the *Official Records* and contemporary Washington, D.C. newspapers attests to a great deal of Confederate guerrilla activity in the surrounding area causing much concern to the Yankees. They attributed it incorrectly to Mosby's Rangers, but Mosby was nearly forty miles away and relatively inactive at this time. In short, Accotink and Alexandria were hotbeds of Confederate guerrillas and spies.

Though we may never know with absolute certainty what Morrow was doing in Accotink, the known facts coupled with circumstantial evidence provide a plausible scenario. Indeed, it is the only logical one. Morrow was carrying a message of great urgency from General J.E.B. Stuart to one of Stuart's intelligence operatives near Alexandria. Stuart was known to possess a superb spy network, and his stable of experienced couriers were apparently unavailable for this assignment. Accordingly, Stuart would have sought a man for this mission who was absolutely dependable, blessed with good judgment, courageous and cool in tense situations and able to operate independently. Stuart must have seen these traits in Morrow.

The next question is this: Was Morrow successful? No incriminating documents were found on him, so he probably delivered Stuart's dispatch and was in the act of departing the area when shot and captured. His service record states he was hospitalized in the D.C. area for a month; sent to Baltimore on August 23, 1863; and exchanged at City Point, Virginia, the next day.

The final question relates specifically to Morrow. Does his subsequent record reflect the same traits Stuart saw in him? Absolutely. Morrow's return to his command immediately on exchange shows he was not one to shirk his soldierly duties. He saw much more hard riding and fighting until his regiment was returned to South Carolina in February 1864. Two months later, Morrow voluntarily left the comparative quiet of the Palmetto State to return to war-torn Virginia to serve as one of Wade Hampton's famed Iron Scouts. He served in this vital and extremely dangerous capacity until the war's end. Morrow neither accepted parole nor took the Oath of Allegiance after the war's end. There can be no doubt whatsoever that Morrow possessed and used all the soldierly attributes Stuart recognized in him.[58]

PRIVATE PETER MANIGAULT: HE GAVE ALL

When war erupted in 1861, men of all ages rushed to serve the Confederacy. It was not unusual to see men in their forties, fifties or even sixties in the army. One of these men was fifty-six-year-old Charlestonian Peter Manigault (pronounced manny-go).

Said to be possessed of wealth and high social position, Manigault was a prosperous planter and Harvard graduate with connections to some of the earliest and most influential families of South Carolina. Nevertheless, he enlisted as a private in the First South Carolina Mounted Militia in 1861. In the spring of 1862, the Confederate army was reorganized and the militia disbanded. At the same time, the age of conscription was set at eighteen to thirty-five. The vast majority of men over thirty-five left the army, but Manigault chose to remain in service by enlisting in the Third South Carolina Cavalry in March 1862.

His company was immediately sent to Grahamville, South Carolina, where it remained until October 1864. It scouted, patrolled and was actively engaged in combat in both battles at Pocotaligo. The service rendered was difficult, tedious and demanding. Apparently, Manigault had no difficulty in keeping up with compatriots many years younger, for otherwise he would have been discharged from the army. That he was retained by his command testifies that he was not a hindrance but a capable and respected soldier despite his age. He must have been truly dedicated to have willfully endured physical hardships, light rations and the rigors of a private in mounted service when he could so easily have resigned from the army at any time and returned to privileged civilian life.

In October 1864, Manigault's command was sent to Georgia to protect a vital railroad connecting Albany and Savannah. A month later, they found themselves facing Sherman's hordes in their infamous March to the Sea. On November 23, Manigault's company was part of about 150 men sent to repel a Union force that had crossed the Oconee River between Augusta and Macon. The Yankees were dislodged and forced back across the river in the ensuing Battle of Ball's Ferry, a small but sharp engagement that halted the Union forward progress for two full days. Confederate casualties were light, with one killed and four wounded. However, among the wounded was Private Peter Manigault, who survived the night but expired the following day.

Manigault's body was returned to his family in Charleston and interred in the French Huguenot Church Cemetery. His death in combat at age fifty-nine makes his story quite remarkable for several reasons. He was under no requirement to have spent a single day in the military. He willingly gave up the ease and comfort of civilian life in service to his new nation. His extended service as one of the oldest men in all the Confederate army is highly commendable and has few parallels. His story, known to but a few, is worthy of remembrance.[59]

Yankees Buried in Magnolia Cemetery: A Desecration

Union soldiers, marines and sailors buried in and around Charleston during the War for Southern Independence were exhumed and reinterred at national cemeteries in Florence and Beaufort shortly after the war. Two men, each a Union officer, were exhumed from Charleston's magnificent Magnolia Cemetery for reinterment in Florence. Their wartime deaths were not so unusual, but the circumstances associated with their burials bring their stories to the forefront.

Marine First Lieutenant Charles H. Bradford was a twenty-three-year-old native of Maine who was wounded and captured in the failed small boat assault on Confederate-held Fort Sumter on the night of September 8–9, 1863. Taken to Charleston's Federal prisoners' hospital, he called for Dr. Albert G. Mackey, a prominent Charlestonian and close friend of Bradford's father through their

U.S. Marine first lieutenant Charles H. Bradford. *Naval History & Heritage Command.*

association with the Freemasons. Mackey was one of the nation's leading members of the Freemasons and is widely known even today for his many influential books and articles on their history. He was also known for his avid Unionist leanings. A newspaper article describes what followed:

> *Dr. Mackey attended to his young friend…with fraternal kindness to his wants, watched by his bedside, and upon his death, which occurred September 23rd, had his body carried to the Masonic Burial Ground in Magnolia Cemetery, where, by himself and his two sons, the only two witnesses to the ceremony, it was consigned to a respectable grave.[60]*

Unfortunately, the good doctor's actions were noticed by the keeper of the cemetery, who reported the unauthorized intrusion to the authorities and others resulting in a great uproar. Dr. Mackey's surreptitious act was fraught with civil and legal implications and liabilities as well as potential consequences from the military for violation of its rules and regulations regarding prisoners. He likely incurred intense protests from his fellow Freemasons for disdaining the principles and rules of their organization with the burial of a non-Mason in their hallowed ground.

Additionally, the cemetery was sacred to Charlestonians for it not only held the graves of numerous local families, but it was the final resting place of many Confederate soldiers as well. Soldiers Ground, a section reserved exclusively for Confederate dead, held the remains of several hundred men who died from disease or wounds received in battles such as Secessionville or Morris Island. Other Confederate soldiers lay buried in family plots scattered throughout the cemetery. The thought of a Yankee being buried in Magnolia Cemetery was simply unheard of. Further, the city and its inhabitants were still in a deep rage at being targeted with indiscriminate shelling from Union guns on Morris Island since the previous month.

All in all, Dr. Mackey was immediately faced with widespread anger and resentment from a multitude of sources for his reckless, impudent and impulsive actions. Whatever penalties were discussed or considered are not known, but in the end, he was punished in a most humiliating manner; he was forced to disinter Bradford's remains, take them to Charleston's potter's field and reinter them there.

In March 1864, U.S. Navy admiral John A. Dahlgren, commander of the South Atlantic Blockading Squadron, learned of the details regarding Bradford's two burials. Dahlgren probably felt some guilt in this matter, for the assault on Fort Sumter was his own idea and about 130 men and officers were killed or captured in that ill-fated assault. Perhaps he personally knew the young marine. Whatever the reason, the potter's field burial for the lieutenant did not sit well with him. Shortly after the fall of Charleston to Union troops in February 1865, he laid plans to remedy what he termed "vindication of the flag and restoring the remains [Bradford's] to the

Union admiral John A. Dahlgren. *Naval History & Heritage Command.*

spot from which they were ejected."[61] He wasted no time in arranging an elaborate reburial with the assistance of Union general John P. Hatch, military commander of Charleston from February to August 1865.

On March 16, 1865, Dahlgren was personally present when Bradford's body was exhumed from the potter's field grave and then went to St. Paul's Church on Coming Street in downtown Charleston for the funeral service. Dahlgren had made certain the church would be filled to near capacity. Attendees included Dahlgren's entire staff, commanding officers of six Union warships in port, General Hatch and his staff, the band of the 21st U.S. Colored Troops, a detachment of the 144th New York Infantry regiment, one hundred sailors, a detachment of marines, a multitude of other naval and army officers and Dr. Mackey's family. When the service concluded, a long funeral procession traveled through Charleston's streets on the two-and-a-half-mile trip to Magnolia Cemetery, where Union authorities had previously secured two cemetery plots. In one, they lay Lieutenant Bradford's remains, and after a short service, a three-volley salute by the marine detachment reverberated across the cemetery.

The newspaper article makes no claim that the final interment for Lieutenant Bradford was in the Masonic section, and cemetery records show the two lots belonged to a Charleston family beforehand. Apparently even Union admirals and generals were reluctant to infringe on the sanctity of Masonic grounds by burying a non-Mason within them. The *Charleston Courier* covered the funeral in a detailed two-column article the next day. From that moment forward though, it appears Lieutenant Bradford was forgotten. Despite the presence and influences of Admiral Dahlgren, General Hatch, Dr. Mackey and other key figures of Union-occupied Charleston, none arranged for a headstone to mark Bradford's grave.

Acting Ensign Joseph S. Johnson, son of Dahlgren's fleet surgeon William Johnson, was one of sixty crewmen killed on January 15, 1865, when their ship, the monitor USS *Patapsco*, struck a torpedo in Charleston's harbor near Fort Moultrie on Sullivan's Island. His body was the only one identified among the final thirteen recovered from the sunken vessel in May 1865. A May 24 newspaper account states all thirteen were interred on James Island without identifying the exact site, but Johnson was actually buried without fanfare in Charleston's Magnolia Cemetery. Cemetery records confirm his interment took place on May 19, 1865, next to Lieutenant Bradford. No newspaper or other accounts of his burial are found.

Magnolia Cemetery's records show Bradford and Johnson were exhumed together in late 1865 for reburial at Florence's new National Cemetery.

Unfortunately, something went awry, for no records are found of either man there. Perhaps the documentation accompanying them was lost or they were diverted elsewhere. However, searches for other burial sites have proven fruitless. Wherever they were reinterred, it seems certain they are reposing with a marker simply stating "Unknown." Each man deserved much better.

7

POSTWAR YEARS AND REMEMBRANCE

Citizens of the South did not forget the men who died in the war or their heroic deeds. Each state devoted itself to gather the fallen dead from battlefield graves within its borders, regardless of the soldier's origins, and provide them a proper grave with a marker. This was nearly always a local task lacking financial or any other support from the Reconstruction state governments. Monuments to the dead and to those who served so honorably began being erected in the 1890s. Again, each was a local effort primarily planned and financed by civilian entities, particularly the United Daughters of the Confederacy and Ladies Memorial Associations. South Carolina was no different.

SOLDIERS GROUND IN MAGNOLIA CEMETERY

Soldiers Ground in beautiful and historic Magnolia Cemetery holds special interest because it is a precious reminder of the sacrifices of those who defended Charleston for nearly four years. Serving as the principal burial location for Confederate servicemen who died in the Charleston area, this section holds the graves of 644 men buried during there during the war. A review of the Ladies Memorial Association of Charleston records of 1881, in which their history and involvement with Magnolia Cemetery were summarized, unveils many details of interest.

Soldier's Ground in Magnolia Cemetery, Charleston South Carolina. *Author's collection.*

Just twenty-eight of these men were officers, all lieutenants or captains. Many corporals and sergeants are identified, but as one would expect, most are privates. They came from all over the Southland. The vast majority are from South Carolina, North Carolina and Georgia, with small numbers from Florida, Virginia, Tennessee and Louisiana. Twenty-four graves are listed as "Unknown," and with the exception of a single sailor from a gunboat, all are from the army.

Two men have the unusual distinction of being noted as "Federal Deserters" who died wearing the gray. Some died in battle, while others, with mortal wounds, lingered in hospitals for varying spells. Most of these casualties were from actions at Secessionville, Battery Wagner and Fort Sumter. However, the majority of those interred in Soldiers Ground died in area hospitals from malaria, smallpox, yellow fever and measles.

The first burial at Soldiers Ground was for Private T.F. Brown, Second South Carolina Artillery, who died on July 16, 1861. The last wartime burials were conducted for 6 "Unknowns," each of whom died on February 24, 1865, shortly after the Union occupation of Charleston. One other man was buried in 1866 under unknown circumstances, and the 80 "Gettysburg Dead" were reinterred in 1871, bringing the total to 725 by that date. A review of wartime burials by year shows 1861, 15 burials; 1862, 158 burials;

1863, 224 burials; 1864, 142 burials; and 1865, 99 burials. There are 6 undated burials. The number of deaths recorded in less than two months of 1865 is staggering and begs an explanation.

Reinterment of 47 Confederate soldiers, sailors and marines recovered from under The Citadel's football stadium in 1999 and 2005 brought the total number of Confederate servicemen at rest in Soldiers Ground to 772. Over 2,500 other Confederate veterans, many of whom were wartime casualties, are at rest in private lots scattered around the cemetery.[62]

Return of the Gettysburg Dead

Soldiers Ground is now the final resting place for nearly eight hundred Confederate soldiers, sailors and marines from eight different states, most of whom died in defense of Charleston. The last row to the left of the central monument is different, not for its outwardly appearance but because it holds the remains of South Carolina's Gettysburg dead. The full story of their return is one that should be appreciated and promoted by all. Their recovery, two years in the making, was achieved only after overcoming a gauntlet of major impediments.

To place things in proper context, one must start in March 1866 with the formation of the Ladies Memorial Association of Charleston, the first such organization of its kind in the South. Its president, Mary Snowden, was a truly dynamic and remarkable lady. At that time, 644 soldiers and a single sailor were buried in Soldiers Ground, none with a headstone. The Ladies had three goals: caring for those graves, providing headstones for each and erecting a suitable monument to their memory.

They enjoyed great support and success in the following months. A grant of $1,000 from the South Carolina General Assembly was received as seed money for the projects. The General Assembly also gifted the association ownership of the unused granite and marble from the recently completed capitol building in Columbia to be used as headstones and monuments in Magnolia Cemetery. The Ladies raised another $700 and were deep in planning when disaster struck in March 1867 with the implementation of Reconstruction. The duly elected governor and General Assembly were thrown out of office and replaced by carpetbaggers, scalawags and their minions. Further, the bank holding the funds of the association was seized by federal authorities, thus preventing the association from accessing their funds.

Accordingly, the granite and marble, still in Columbia, could not be moved for lack of funds. These devastating blows brought the work of the Ladies to a screeching halt. For two years, little could be done as Reconstruction ravaged South Carolina, causing the Palmetto State to become better known as the Prostrate State.

In April 1869, much news emerged from Gettysburg. The superintendent of the new National Cemetery there advised that fewer than 700 of the estimated 3,700 Confederate strewn around in the fields of Gettysburg could be identified. By then, all Union soldiers buried in and around Gettysburg had been recovered and moved to the new national cemetery there. However, the men in gray remained in the same scattered shallow graves they had occupied for six years. Threats by locals to desecrate the remains of the Confederate dead filtered in. Gettysburg farmers were threatening to plow up their remains and use their bones as fertilizer.

While some decried these conditions, many northern newspapers and politicians fully supported the depredations proposed by the farmers. A couple of sympathetic northerners in Congress, disgusted by this situation, put forth a proposal for the U.S. government to purchase five acres near the battlefield for use as a Confederate cemetery but their efforts received no backing.

Gettysburg resident Samuel Weaver was instrumental in the recovery of Union soldiers from the battlefield and, while doing that work, recorded the location of each Confederate grave site he found. In 1869, he announced he could identify the graves of sixty South Carolinians. All this news reinvigorated the association. They vowed to gather these men and bring them home. At the same time, they set about restarting their original plans for Soldiers Ground.

In 1870, Mary Snowden traveled to Gettysburg to meet with Samuel Weaver and the national cemetery superintendent. She learned that many Confederate dead lay within the borders of the national cemetery and could not be removed without authorization of U.S. Army quartermaster general Montgomery Meigs, who was in charge of all national cemeteries. Meigs was hostile to anyone and anything connected with the Confederacy. He prohibited placement of flowers on Confederate graves in Arlington as late as 1882, when he finally retired. Mary Snowden visited Meigs and asked permission to remove the South Carolinians but was bluntly refused. She conveyed this to Samuel Weaver, who took it upon himself to communicate directly with General Meigs on her behalf. His personal exertions over several months eventually won Meigs's approval for Confederates from any state to

Mary Snowden, the guiding force of the Ladies Memorial Association of Charleston, South Carolina. *Image from* Memorials to the Memory of Mary Amarintha Snowden.

be removed. This victory was welcomed, but another hurdle was yet to be cleared.

Some Gettysburg farmers were demanding an exorbitant amount of money before allowing access to the soldiers buried on their properties and appointed one of their number as their spokesman. Mary Snowden called on him at his house to seek recovery of the men without payment of this ransom. The farmer was adamant that it must be paid, and their conversation turned into a lengthy debate, with neither backing down. The matter was unexpectedly settled when the farmer's wife influenced her husband to let Mary Snowden have those men without charge. He acquiesced and withdrew demand of payment. The door for other Southern states to recover their fallen men was now opened.

In February 1871, several major events occurred. The Ladies sponsored a fair in Charleston that raised almost $1,700, more than enough to pay for exhumation in Gettysburg and reinterment in Soldiers Ground. At the same time, Mary Snowden somehow convinced South Carolina's carpetbagger governor to ship the marble and granite from Columbia to Charleston at no cost to the association. This meant a headstone for each man in Soldiers Ground could now be prepared. But shortly afterward, Samuel Weaver was killed in an accident, leaving return of the Gettysburg dead in great jeopardy. Fortunately, Weaver's son Dr. Rufus Weaver stepped forward just a few days later. Advising that he was familiar with his father's work, he pledged to provide the assistance promised by his father and soon announced that eighty-four men could be identified as South Carolinians.

In April 1871, Mary Snowden and several members of the Memorial Association departed for Gettysburg with confidence. Dr. Weaver worked quickly to have the South Carolinians exhumed. The remains were carefully placed in seventy numbered boxes. Sixty-eight boxes each held the remains of a single soldier. Two graves, one holding the remains of seven men and the other nine, filled the other two boxes. Since the individuals in them could not be distinguished one from another they were kept together in the same manner as they were buried. The boxes left Gettysburg for Baltimore, where they were quickly sent by ship to Charleston for reinterment in their native soil. The costs for inland transportation to Baltimore and ocean transportation to Charleston were paid for by anonymous sympathetic citizens of Baltimore.

Four sets of remains were immediately claimed by relatives and buried in family plots elsewhere in Magnolia Cemetery. On May 10, 1871, just a couple of weeks after leaving Gettysburg, the other eighty men were laid to rest in Soldiers Ground. Schools and most businesses closed early that day to allow folks to attend. All sources state that over six thousand people were present for the service.

The *Charleston Daily News* provided a lengthy article on the service the following day. One paragraph in particular stands out. It read:

> *While the ode was being sung, the open graves were being filled up, after which the Ladies of the Memorial Association began the work of decorating the graves. On each was placed a chaplet, frequently varied by colorful crosses of evergreen and flowers. Not one was forgotten, and the tender and loving manner with which the work was done showed the deep feelings of the fair decorators. In the center of the burial-ground was a large evergreen cross, covered with white lilies, and standing upon a raised mound. It formed a beautiful central figure and emblem to the lowly graves around. The remains which were re-interred are not yet furnished with headstones but this will be attended to shortly.*[63]

Those reinterred came from every corner of the Palmetto State. Over thirty different enlistment sites were identified. They came from all walks of life—teachers, farmers, tradesmen, planters, clerks, students, merchants, a physician and a prominent newspaperman. Some were sons from wealthy families, one was an orphan and two were brothers. The records indicate no more than perhaps twenty were married. Many died on the battlefield itself, others in Confederate or Union hospitals.

By Memorial Day the next year, headstones were in place for the Gettysburg dead as well as the other 645 men in Soldiers Ground. The primary missions of Mary Snowden and the Ladies Memorial Association were nearly complete. The monument in the center of Soldiers Ground was erected several years later after much planning and long-term fundraising.

South Carolinians were the first to be removed from Gettysburg. With the path cleared of obstacles by Mary Snowden and the invaluable assistance of Samuel Weaver and his son along with a certain farmer's wife, North Carolina recovered 137 of its men and Georgia reclaimed 101 of its own. Virginia took all the others unclaimed by states or family and re-interred them at Richmond's Hollywood Cemetery.

Hollywood Cemetery later advised that among those they received were twenty-six other South Carolinians that had been missed by the Weavers. A Charleston newspaper later acknowledged Virginia's magnanimous actions with a statement reading in part: "For the loving care with which they have held the sacred bones of our dead, the people of the whole South owe [the Virginians] a debt of everlasting gratitude. South Carolina, at least, will never forget what they have done for our fallen sons."[64]

The 150th anniversary of the return of South Carolina's Gettysburg dead was observed at Soldiers Ground on Confederate Memorial Day 2021. Their story was presented, and a monument dedicated to all the South Carolinians at the Battle of Gettysburg was unveiled. Full credit for the recovery of every single Confederate soldier from the fields of Gettysburg, regardless of his state, is due to the untiring efforts of the Ladies Memorial Association of Charleston. They were the ones who overcame the challenges of bringing those men back to Southern soil when no else could or would.

Last Mission of the Iron Scouts

The War for Southern Independence ended in 1865, but for one South Carolinian, it didn't become final until he performed one last mission. Few stories from the immediate postwar years can match the compassion and kindness it carries.

Private William Wallace Miller, son of an Aiken planter, enlisted in Confederate service in Hamburg, South Carolina, on September 1861 at age eighteen. His company became part of the First South Carolina Cavalry and saw much action in Virginia. Miller was recognized as a superb soldier, confident, cool and brave under fire. These attributes led to his appointment as one of Wade Hampton's Iron Scouts in early 1863. Miller is found in numerous accounts in which he displayed courage, daring and resourcefulness. Bad luck led to his capture on November 15, 1864, and he was sent to Point Lookout as a prisoner of war.

Private Solomon E. Legare, from the family of a Charleston planter, enlisted in Confederate service on April 15, 1861, at age twenty-one. His company later became part of the Sixth South Carolina Cavalry, which arrived in Virginia in May 1864. Legare showed great mettle, courage and, like Wallace Miller, the rare ability to remain cool and unfazed while in close combat. These attributes led to his regimental commander appointing him to Hampton's Iron Scouts in late September 1864. Legare was described as "a splendid fellow, gentle, courteous and brave."[65] Unfortunately, he had the misfortune of suffering an ankle wound and being captured about six weeks later. Sent to Point Lookout prison camp, he reunited with Miller.

Private Wallace Miller of the First South Carolina Cavalry and a member of Wade Hampton's Iron Scouts. *From* Butler and His Cavalry in the War of Secession, 1861–1865.

Miller and Legare languished together through the harsh winter of 1864–65 and watched as many others imprisoned there died. Legare's wound apparently left him crippled and sickly, for he was slated for exchange in mid-March 1865. However, that exchange never occurred, and he was not officially released until June 28. Miller was officially released a day later. However, neither man was physically capable of leaving because each had come down with acute dysentery, a disease that killed many during the war.

Legare did not fare well at all. Miller recovered shortly afterward, but instead of leaving Point Lookout, he stayed to nurse and encourage Legare. Sadly, Legare died on July 22 after several weeks of suffering. Only then did Miller begin his trek back to home.

Miller never forgot his friend and compatriot. In 1868, on his own volition, he returned to Point Lookout, claimed Legare's remains and brought them back to Legare's family in Charleston. This last mission, guided by the principles of respect, tenderness and mercy, quietly closed the book on the Iron Scouts. It is a credit to Wallace Miller that despite his many wartime experiences, full of danger and death, and living through the vile conditions of Point Lookout, he emerged from the war without loss of his Christian principles while maintaining his faithfulness to a brother in arms.[66]

SOUTH CAROLINA'S UNITED CONFEDERATE VETERANS

The United Confederate Veterans organization was formed in 1889, almost a quarter of a century after Appomattox. Consisting of men who had served in the Confederate army, navy or marines, their goals were noble and visionary. The UCV Constitution emphatically stated that it was to be a "Social, Literary, Historical and Benevolent" organization. One goal was for members to gather wartime material (i.e., maps, rosters, correspondence, records, etc.) and write accounts of their military service so that "an impartial and historically accurate history of the Confederate side" of the war could be presented and preserved. Another called for the erection of monuments for "our great leaders and heroic soldiers and people" and "marking with suitable headstones the graves of Confederate dead wherever found." Yet another goal was the care of disabled and destitute former Confederate servicemen as well as needy widows and orphans of men who honorably wore the Gray.

The last goal mentioned in the UCV Constitution looked far into the future. It reads: "To instill in our descendants a proper veneration for the spirit and glory of their fathers, and bring them into association with our organization, that they may aid us in accomplishing our objects and purposes, and finally succeed us, and take up our work where we may leave it." This ultimately led to the establishment of the Sons of Confederate Veterans in 1896.

The UCV grew rapidly from its inception. In 1896, it boasted 850 camps across the South and elsewhere, including Illinois, Washington, D.C., Montana, New Mexico, California, Indiana and Canada. South Carolina had eighty-seven camps. The Stephen Elliott Camp no. 51 in St. George was the state's first chartered UCV camp. Camp Sumter no. 250 was the first in Charleston. Urban centers such as Charleston, Columbia and Greenville had multiple camps. Many, however, came from smaller towns and communities like Moncks Corner, Ninety-Six, Jennys, Due West, Glymphville and Hyman.

Over 160,000 Confederate veterans were members at one time or another with a total of 1,885 camps being chartered. In 1903, 1,523 active camps were on the rolls, 136 of them from South Carolina. From that year on, the number of camps gradually decreased as members died. The need for the Sons of Confederate Veterans to join in their work was formally recognized in 1906 by the UCV. At that point the Sons stepped forward to add their strength and numbers to cooperate with the UCV in support of their missions.

UCV membership zeal and fidelity never wavered. In 1921, when the youngest members were in their mid-seventies, the number of active UCV camps was surprisingly strong at 1,020, with 55 from the Palmetto State.[67]

MAJOR WILLIAM ELLIOTT: A LASTING LEGACY

William Elliott (1838–1907), a member of the prominent Elliott family from Beaufort, is a man especially deserving of our gratitude and respect. A prewar attorney, he was among five brothers who served in the Confederate army, one of whom was Brigadier General Stephen Elliott Jr. Their father served as an army chaplain at one point of the war.

William enlisted shortly after South Carolina seceded from the Union. After he was elected first lieutenant, he and his company were sent to Virginia in May 1862 as part of the Second Palmetto Regiment. That summer, his company was converted from infantry to light artillery and served with distinction in a number of engagements. Elliott was sent west after having been promoted to captain and appointed assistant adjutant general on the staff of General Stephen Dill Lee, a position he held until the war's end.

Elliott was twice cited for battlefield heroism despite his position as a senior staff officer. At Champions Hill, after picking up a fallen regimental flag, he carried it through the raging battle, exposing himself to prolonged heavy fire while inspiring those around him. At Vicksburg, after a Union assault captured a vital trench line, he led a counter-attack using lighted twelve-pound cannon balls as grenades to drive the enemy away. For his heroism and superb leadership, he was promoted to major. Following the war's end, he returned to his law practice and, as a Democrat, served several terms as a U.S. congressman from South Carolina.

His war record, impressive as it was, is overshadowed by his work after retiring from Congress. In 1906, President Teddy Roosevelt appointed Elliott the U.S. commissioner in charge of marking Confederate graves in cemeteries at or near former U.S. prisoner-of-war camps in the North. Elliott took this assignment quite seriously, devoting his full attention and energy to carrying out his charge. He traveled to every known site in numerous states, recorded names and locations of those interred and set in place the process of obtaining and erecting headstones for those Confederate dead. The first set of markers went to Elmira, New York, and the second set was delivered to Camp Chase, Ohio.

Tragically, William Elliott died suddenly in 1907. However, the zeal, drive and intensity he placed in his work set the standard for completion of this vital project under others following his guidelines and examples. What he accomplished in his one year of service on this project was simply remarkable and makes him worthy of remembrance.[68]

CHARLESTON'S DEFENDERS MONUMENT

White Point Garden, Charleston

Millions of people touring Charleston over the years have enjoyed the beautiful and scenic view of the harbor and enjoyed the shade of White Point Garden. Most have stopped to read the inscriptions of the various monuments there, the most prominent being the *Confederate Defenders of Charleston* monument. This wonderful work of art is an acknowledgement of the heroism of those defending Fort Sumter successfully against Union threats from 1863 to 1865, a feat worthy of the highest respect from those familiar with its story.

The monument was several years in planning and fundraising. Native Charlestonian Andrew Buist Murray (1844–1928) bequeathed to the City of Charleston $100,000 for the monument, thus ensuring its completion and placement. Murray, orphaned as a youngster, served in a fire engine company during the war that was often called on for military service all around Charleston. Twice he served on the lines at James Island and was under fire numerous times. His postwar career as a businessman brought him great wealth, which he generously shared. In his lifetime, he donated over $1 million to the city, The Citadel, the College of Charleston, the Seaman's Home and numerous other recipients both public and private.

The monument was officially unveiled and presented on October 20, 1932. The *Charleston News and Courier* had its story on the front page the next day. Over eight thousand people were in attendance. The story stated, "Many present had fathers, uncles and grandfathers who had fought in the...war." The Corps of Cadets from The Citadel was present along with the Sumter Guards and the Washington Light Infantry. Among the special guests and speakers was William Robert Greer, a Charleston resident and the last living Confederate veteran of Fort Sumter. Greer served as a private in Company B (Washington Light Infantry), Twenty-

Fifth South Carolina Infantry, and was at Battery Wagner as part of its last garrison before it was evacuated on September 7, 1863. He and his company became part of Sumter's garrison for about thirty days in October and endured the initial stages of the Second Great Bombardment of the fort. He returned for another stint there in February 1864. A true and faithful soldier, he was captured at Fort Fisher, North Carolina, in January 1865 but survived Elmira prisoner-of-war camp until release the following June.

When the army evacuated Charleston in February 1865, Sumter's final commander, Captain Thomas A. Huguenin, carried the last Confederate flag to fly over the fort with him. Passed along to the Sumter Guards for posterity purposes after the war, it was presented and used in the monument dedication. The actual unveiling was performed by, as reported in the newspaper article, "four young ladies, all descendants of members of the Confederate garrison of the fort." One was a granddaughter of Colonel Alfred Rhett, the first commanding officer. Another was granddaughter of Captain Huguenin, and another was granddaughter of Major John Johnson, the premier engineer at Sumter in its darkest days. The fourth lady was a grandniece of General Stephen Elliott, the fort's commander from September 1863 to May 1864. Each of these officers is credited with inspiring leadership in perilous times and earned great acclaim for their service at the fort.

The *Defenders* monument was presented in the early years of the Great Depression. Intended to provide recognition and respect for those who endured so much in the defense of Fort Sumter, it has served as an inspiration to later generations. Its dedication was meaningful to the city and its residents then and remains so today.

Torpedo Boatmen Memorial

White Point Garden, Charleston, South Carolina

The *Defenders* monument on Charleston's Battery is the most widely recognized and visible monument in Charleston. Close by but less familiar is another Confederate-themed monument in White Point Garden, the Torpedo Boatmen Memorial. It has long been overlooked and rarely noted in recent years, but it should be an inspiration to all.

On January 11, 1899, the *Charleston Evening Post* reported the United Daughters of the Confederacy had petitioned the City of Charleston for permission to place a memorial tablet in city hall to the memory of the men of the Confederate Torpedo Service. The idea was readily accepted, but later discussion led to other possible placement sites. In time the concept grew much larger, and a decision was made to erect a suitable monument instead of simply placing a memorial tablet on a wall. With this in mind, a location in White Point Garden at the foot of Meeting Street was selected. The UDC and the Ladies Memorial Association of Charleston joined forces and worked closely with the city in making the monument a reality less than four months after the initial concept was presented.

The Ladies Memorial Association quietly appealed for $1,000 in donations to cover the cost, which was quickly met, with nearly every dollar coming from Charlestonians. A fine piece of granite allowing for a seven-foot-tall monument was donated from a firm in Greenville, and the sculptor added flanking water fountains in the form of dolphins. The southern face has a detailed brass plaque attesting to its purpose, with the top portion reading, "In Memory of the Supreme Devotion of Those Heroic Men of the Confederate Army and Navy, First in Maritime Warfare to Employ Torpedo Boats 1863–1865." The memorial tablet mentions *Torch, Hunley* and the *Little David* as well as the then-known names of those who died in their service. It also mentions some of their specific attacks against the Union fleet blockading Charleston.

The *Charleston News and Courier* carried a lengthy article on May 9, 1899, following the monument dedication. Headlined "Long Neglected Heroes, Fitting Honor Done Their Memories Yesterday," it reported a festive occasion with martial music, a Confederate flag and much enthusiasm. The timing of this event was particularly notable, for May 9 was the start of the United Confederate Veterans Convention in Charleston and thousands of UCV members were in the city.

Simple in design and appearance, its meaning and significance have never changed or been diminished. By all accounts, the men in the Torpedo Service were heroic volunteers deserving proper recognition for their efforts in one of the most dangerous fields of duty in the war.

Housatonic, Hunley and Lieutenant Dixon Sail Again

Lieutenant George E. Dixon, commander of the *Hunley*, would never have dreamed his name and that of his vessel would be given to ships in the U.S. Navy. He and the *Hunley* had their names etched in history when *Hunley* sank the USS *Housatonic* off Charleston's coast on February 17, 1864, in the world's first successful submarine attack. Yet the U.S. Navy acknowledged and honored both ships and Dixon in its most profound way by naming later ships for them.

The second *Housatonic* (SP-1697) was a civilian freighter/ passenger vessel. Built by Southern Pacific Steamship Company in 1899 under the name *El Rio*, it was taken over by the navy and renamed as the United States entered World War I. Converted to a minelayer and sailing from Scotland, *Housatonic* laid over nine thousand mines in the North Sea and, after the war ended, made three trips returning U.S. troops home from Europe. Returned to its civilian owners in 1919, it was renamed *Brazos* and continued in commercial service until lost in a collision at sea in 1942.

Submarine tender USS *Hunley* (AS-31). *Naval History & Heritage Command.*

The third *Housatonic* (A0-35) was a new tanker, the SS *ESSO Albany*, built by Standard Oil Company in 1941 and converted into a fleet oiler early in World War II under its new name. Serving as a workhorse, it earned five battle stars while supporting the fleet with service in the Atlantic, Mediterranean and Pacific theaters of war. Its navy service began in January 1942 and ended in March 1946 when it was returned to its owners. Afterward, it sailed under various names and ownerships until the 1990s.

The USS *Hunley* was designed and built specifically as a submarine tender. Designated AS-31, the USS *Hunley* provided superb service from 1961 to 1994 supporting Polaris and Poseidon submarines. Far different than the spar-torpedo boat size and configuration of the original *Hunley*, it was christened by the wife of Charleston's mayor J. Palmer Gaillard. Home-ported variously at Charleston, Holy Loch, Guam and Norfolk, USS *Hunley* earned many awards during its thirty-three years of active service. After being decommissioned, it was sold for scrap.

The ship named after Lieutenant George E. Dixon was the USS *Dixon* (AS-37). It, too, was designed and built for service as a submarine tender.

Submarine tender USS *Dixon* (AS-37). *Naval History & Heritage Command.*

Its twenty-four years of service (1971–1995) were mostly spent in the Pacific while home-ported in San Diego. *Dixon* provided excellent support for the U.S. Fleet Ballistic Missile submarine fleet and, surprisingly, was involved in Operation Desert Storm. Following its decommissioning, it was used as a target and sunk in a training exercise.[69]

EPILOGUE

The stories and topics covered in this work represent only a fraction of events on South Carolina's soil or actions involving its men. Those presented within these pages were selected as they best represent the wide scope of available subject matter of the state's hidden history. Some readers might call the contents trivial affairs, but to those directly involved, they were major in every way, particularly those involving life or death situations. Such stories and most topics are not taught in schools, seminars or any other public venue. A book like this one is the only source for all but the most dedicated researcher.

For me, as a historian, a southerner and especially a South Carolinian, the War for Southern Independence holds great interest. It is a topic all Americans should study. Not only do we learn about the past, but we learn how it shaped the present as well. We can gain a greater appreciation of our heritage and culture. We can also acquire inspiration to face today's challenges by studying how South Carolinians resolutely overcame the difficulties and hardships they encountered in this period.

D.M.T.

NOTES

1. South Carolina in Overview: 1861–1865

1. *War of the Rebellion: A Compilation of the Official Records of Union and Confederate Armies*, 44:743. Hereafter cited as *OR* and unless otherwise noted taken from series 1.

2. The Early Days

2. *OR*, 1:236–39, 241–42. *Courier*, April 6, 1861; *Mercury*, April 6, 1861.
3. Rosen and Hatcher, *First Shot*, 59; Doubleday, *Reminiscences of Forts Sumter and Moultrie*, 22–23, 176–77, 185; for Richard Kidder Meade Jr., *Compiled Service Records of Confederate General and Staff Officers and Nonregimental Enlisted Men, 1861–1865*, M331, Roll 109.
4. Doubleday, *Reminiscences of Forts Sumter and Moultrie*, 171–72; Rosen and Hatcher, *First Shot*, 58–59; *OR*, 1:66–67.
5. South Carolina Department of Archives and History, "Coast Police Accounts and Vouchers, 1861–1864" and "Coast Police Reports, 1861–1862," Record Group Number 126000, Series Numbers. S 166181 and. S 126205. The Koszta Affair, for which Duncan gained his international recognition, is well documented in multiple sources; Navy History and Heritage Command, https://www.history.navy.mil.
6. *Official Records of the Union and Confederate Navies*, series 1, 4:260–61. Hereafter cited as *OR Navies* and series 1 unless otherwise noted.

7. Krick, *Staff Officers in Gray*, 10–14, 95–96; *OR*, 1:18, 1:35–36 and other references in this chapter; Alexander Chisolm Papers, MS 5002, the New York Historical Society; *Compiled Service Records of Confederate General and Staff Officers, and Non-Regimental Enlisted Men, 1861–1865*, Pub. M331, Record Group 109, Roll 0054. He is occasionally referenced as lieutenant colonel, the South Carolina militia rank given him when he was an aide to Governor Pickens,

8. *Mercury*, May 21, July 2 and July 16, 1861; "In the Court of the Confederate States-District of South Carolina," *Mercury*, August 3, 1861; "News of the Day," *New York Times*, August 29, 1861; *OR Navies*, 1, 6:6, 6:181–82.

3. Leadership

9. Ohio State University Department of History, "Joseph Brevard Kershaw," https://history.osu.edu.

10. *Compiled Service Records*, M267 Roll 0363; M331, Roll 0043.

11. Ibid.

12. Brooks, *Butler and His Cavalry*, 11, 387.

13. Ohio State University Department of History, "Joseph Brevard Kershaw."

14. *Compiled Service Records*, M267, Roll 0156; M331, Roll 0148.

15. *OR*, 36, 1062; Longstreet, *From Manassas to Appomattox*, 564.

16. *Compiled Service Records*, M267, Roll 0367; M331, Roll 0159.

17. The primary source for this listing is an email to the author dated February 2, 2023, from the South Caroliniana Library, University of South Carolina, listing its graduate generals.

18. Chisolm, *Manual of Military Surgery*, preface.

19. Civil Practice to Civil War, "Introduction," https://waring.library.musc.edu/exhibits/civilwar/.

20. CSA War Department, "List of Appointments."

21. *OR*, 28:39–40.

22. *Compiled Service Records*, M267, Roll 0105.

23. Ibid.

24. *OR*, 28:189; 35:176.

25. Stephen Elliott has four separate sets of Compiled Service Records, each filled with multiple accounts of his activities and holding letters of commendation relating to his military service. Despite a wealth of information within them, only a single book has ever been written on him.

See D. Michael Thomas, *Confederate General Stephen Elliott: Beaufort Legend, Charleston Hero.*

4. Blockade of South Carolina's Coast

26. This was just one of several violations of international law by the Lincoln government involving his navy. Others include the sinking of the two "Stone Fleets" in Charleston's harbor entrance, the "*Trent* Affair" and the seizure of Confederate commerce raider CSS *Florida* while in a Brazilian port.
27. Many resources were accessed for this chapter. Steven Wise's *Lifeline of the Confederacy* is generally considered the best on the overall blockade. Rick Simmons's *Defending South Carolina's Coast* (2009) is the first known work pertaining to the sites above Charleston, while Tracy Enzor's 2021 thesis is the only other known effort to document them. Other sources include a lengthy and informative telephone conversation on February 19, 2022, with historian Ben Burroughs of Coastal Carolina University, an authority on Horry County and its history. The vast majority of what is found on blockade-running activities above Charleston comes from reports of Union naval officers found by the dozens in *OR Navies* volumes 13–16. Another invaluable source is Marcus Prine's "Ships That Tested the Blockade of the Carolina Ports."

5. Naval Operations: 1861–1865

28. Stone, "Confederate Defense of Charleston," provides a superb analysis of problems facing the Union fleet there. As a naval lieutenant commander, Stone's thesis was submitted to the U.S. Army Command and General Staff College at Fort Leavenworth, Kansas, to satisfy a part of his master's degree in military arts and science. It is available online: https://apps.dtic.mil/sti/tr/pdf/ADA258517.pdf.
29. "Brilliant Naval Exploit," *Courier*, August 7, 1863; "Capture of a Yankee Launch," *Mercury*, August 7, 1863.
30. *OR Navies*, 14:427.
31. *OR Navies*, 14:425–26.
32. *OR Navies*, 14:498–500, 14:761, 15:231.
33. *OR*, 35:8–9, 35:396-400.

34. *OR Navies*, 16:190–94; *OR*, 47, pt. 2, 151–56.
35. *OR*, 35, pt. 1, 21; 35, pt. 2, 225.

6. Soldiers' Stories

36. Austin, *General John Bratton*, 92.
37. Ibid., 92–94.
38. *OR*, 14:271, 273; *Compiled Service Records*, M267, Roll 0113.
39. Brooks, *Butler and His Cavalry*, 67.
40. Ibid., 308.
41. Lieutenant General Wade Hampton III, "The Connected Narrative of Wade Hampton III," Hampton Family Papers, South Caroliniana Library, University of South Carolina, Columbia, SC.
42. Brooks, *Butler and His Cavalry*, 147.
43. Henderson, *Autobiography of Arab*, 64–71; *Charleston Daily Courier*, February 26, 1863; Thomas, *Wade Hampton's Iron Scouts*, 32–34.
44. Henderson, *Autobiography of Arab*, and Brooks, *Butler and His Cavalry*, are the primary sources pertaining to Wade Hampton's "Iron" Scouts. Written by members of the Scouts, they give firsthand accounts of their service. Henderson covers the first fourteen months of their service while Brooks provides in-depth material extending to the war's end. Thomas's *Wade Hampton's Iron Scouts: Confederate Special Forces* expands their story with the addition of much new information and placing the service of the Scouts in chronological order and historical perspective, something the other books lack.
45. *Compiled Service Records*, M347, Roll 0066; *Confederate Papers Relating to Citizens or Business Firms, 1861–1865*, M 346, Roll 0153; Find a Grave, "Col William Richard Cathcart," https://www.findagrave.com; Cathcart's obituary, November 14, 1898; Johnson, *Defense of Charleston Harbor*, 192.
46. *Compiled Service Records*, M258, Roll 0110.
47. Parker, "Captain Lyle," 165–72; Thomas, "Captain Joseph B. Lyle," 16–19, 51; *Compiled Service Records*, M267, Roll 0194. For a complete description of Lyle's Deed, see "One Captures Six Hundred," *Post and Courier*, October 1, 1905.
48. Franklin K. Huger (1844–1926) was just eighteen years old at the time of Elliott's letter of recommendation. A student at The Citadel in Charleston, he left school, enlisted in the Sixth South Carolina Cavalry and was ultimately detached to the Signal Corps. In the summer of 1864,

he was commissioned a second lieutenant in the First South Carolina Infantry. Elliott's letter was misfiled and is found in the *Compiled Service Record* of Lieutenant O.N. Butler, M267, Roll 109; also, Johnson, *Defense of Charleston*, 144, 161.

49. Taft, "Signal Service Corps," 130–34; Cummins, "Signal Corps in the Confederate States Army," 93–107; Emerson and Stokes provide wonderful coverage of the service of Augustine T. Smythe, a member of the Signal Corps in Charleston, in their book *Days of Destruction*. A review of the Compiled Service Records for many of the known Signal Corps operators provides additional details to their service.

50. *OR*, 35, pt. 1, 201; *Compiled Service Records*, M267, Roll 0085.

51. *Compiled Service Records*, M267, Roll 0121.

52. Hitt and Capers, "Flag of the Twelfth Georgia Artillery," 113.

53. *OR*, 35, pt. 1, 184–85.

54. Thomas, *Wade Hampton's Iron Scouts*, 43, 47, 49, 54, 58–59; Brooks, *Butler and His Cavalry*, 98–99; *OR*, 29, pt. 1, 496–98; *Compiled Service Records*, M267, Roll 0001.

55. *OR*, 28, pt. 1, 171, 641; *OR*, pt. 2, 555.

56. Longstreet, *From Manassas to Appomattox*, 254–55.

57. *OR*, 14:280-4; *Daily News*, April 29, 1863.

58. *Compiled Service Records*, M267, Roll 0012.

59. Ibid.

60. "Funeral of Lieut. Charles H. Bradford," *Courier*, March 17, 1865.

61. Ibid.

7. Postwar Years and Remembrance

62. Porcher, *Brief History of the Ladies Association*. Porcher includes the complete burial list at Magnolia as well as an abundance of detail on Confederate dead elsewhere in Charleston; "Our Dead at Gettysburg," *Daily Phoenix*, July 12, 1866; "The Confederate Dead at Gettysburg," *Tarboro Southerner*, April 15, 1869; "An Appeal for the Removal of Confederate Dead at Gettysburg," *Wilmington Journal*, October 15, 1869; "From the Wires," *Daily News*, November 1, 1869; "The Confederate Dead," *Daily News*, April 4, 1870; "Our Dead at Gettysburg," *Daily News*, June 20, 1870; "The Confederate Dead at Gettysburg," *Daily Phoenix*, February 5, 1871; "The Memorial Fair," *Daily News*, March 2, 1871; "The South Carolina Dead at Gettysburg," *Fairfield Herald*, April 26, 1872; "Memorial Celebration,"

Daily News, May 11, 1871; "The North Carolina Dead at Gettysburg," *Wilmington Journal,* September 15, 1871; "Memorial Day," *Daily News,* May 6, 1872; "South Carolina Soldiers Interred at Hollywood," *Daily News,* June 25, 1872.

63. "Memorial Celebration," *Daily News,* May 11, 1871.

64. "South Carolina Soldiers Interred at Hollywood," *Daily News,* June 25, 1872.

65. Brooks, *Butler and His Cavalry,* 513.

66. Ibid., 418, 513; *Compiled Service Records,* M267, Rolls 0005, 0042.

67. "Organization of Camps in the United Confederate Veterans," 1896 through 1921 issues.

68. *Compiled Service Records,* M331, Roll 0085; findagrave.com; ancestry.com.

69. NavSource Naval History, https://www.navsource.org/archives/; Navy History and Heritage Command, https://www.history.navy.mil.

BIBLIOGRAPHY

Books and Articles

Austin, J. Luke. *General John Bratton: Sumter to Appomattox in Letters to His Wife*. Sewanee, TN: Proctor's Hall Press, 2003.

Brooks, U.R. *Butler and His Cavalry in the War of Secession, 1861–1865*. Columbia, SC: State Company, 1909.

Chisolm, Julian John. *Manual of Military Surgery*. Columbia, SC: Evans & Cogswell, 1861.

Cummins, Edmund H. "The Signal Corps in the Confederate States Army." *Southern Historical Society Papers* 16 (1888): 93–107.

Doubleday, Abner. *Reminiscences of Forts Sumter and Moultrie in 1860–1862*. New York: Harper and Brothers, 1876.

Emerson, W. Eric, and Karen Stokes. *Days of Destruction*. Columbia: University of South Carolina Press, 2017.

Enzor, Tracy. "Blockade Runners During the Civil War: Murrell's Inlet and Little River, South Carolina." Master's thesis, Liberty University, Lynchburg, Virginia, 2021.

Girardeau, John L. *Confederate Memorial Day, Charleston S.C. Re-Interment of the Carolina Dead from Gettysburg*. Charleston, SC: William G. Mazyck, Printer, 1871.

Hampton Family Papers, South Caroliniana Library, University of South Carolina, Columbia, South Carolina.

Henderson, E. Prioleau. *Autobiography of Arab*. Columbia, SC: R.L . Bryan Company, 1901.

Hitt, W.H., and H.D. Capers. "Flag of the Twelfth Georgia Artillery." *Confederate Veteran* 16 (1908): 113.

Johnson, John. *The Defense of Charleston Harbor Including Fort Sumter and the Adjacent Islands 1863–1865*. Charleston, SC: Walker, Evans & Cogswell, 1890.

Krick, Robert E.L. *Staff Officers in Gray*. Chapel Hill: University of North Carolina Press, 2003.

Leader, Jonathon, and Randy Burbage. "Humanitarian Exhumation at the Citadel's Johnson Hagood Stadium." *Legacy* 5, no. 1 (2000): 1, 4–7.

Longstreet, James. *From Manassas to Appomattox*. Philadelphia, PA: J.B. Lippincott, 1896.

O'Flaherty, Daniel. "The Blockade That Failed." *American Heritage Magazine* 6, no. 5 (August 1955).

Parker, Elmer O. "Captain Lyle: Forgotten Hero of the Confederacy." *Prologue: The Journal of the National Archives* 4, no. 3 (Fall 1972): 165–72.

Porcher, F.A. *A Brief History of the Ladies Memorial Association of Charleston, SC*. Charleston, SC: H.P Cooke & Co., 1880.

Price, Marcus W. "Ships That Tested the Blockade of the Carolina Ports." *American Neptune Magazine*, July 1948.

Rosen, Robert N., and Richard W. Hatcher III. *The First Shot*. Charleston, SC: Arcadia Publishing, 2011.

Simmons, Rick. *Defending South Carolina's Coast*, Charleston, SC: The History Press, 2009.

Stone, Howard L. "The Confederate Defense of Charleston, South Carolina." Master's thesis, State University of New York Maritime College, Bronx, New York, 1992.

Taft, A.W. "The Signal Service Corps, C.S.A." *Southern Historical Society Papers* 25 (1897): 130–34.

Thomas, D. Michael. "Captain Joseph Banks Lyle." *Confederate Veteran*, July/August 2005.

———. *Confederate General Stephen Elliott: Beaufort Legend, Charleston Hero*. Charleston SC: The History Press, 2020.

———. *Wade Hampton's Iron Scouts: Confederate Special Forces*. Charleston, SC: The History Press, 2018.

Wilcox, Arthur M., and Warren Ripley. *The Civil War at Charleston, a Post-Courier Booklet*. Charleston, SC: News and Courier and Evening Post, 1975.

Wise, Stephen R. *Lifeline of the Confederacy*. Columbia: University of South Carolina Press, 1988.

Archival Depositories

Ancestry | ancestry.com

Confederate Veteran Magazine | 40 volumes. Nashville, TN, 1892–1932.

CSA War Department. "List of Appointments Made from the Ranks, From the Exhibition of Distinguished Valor and Skill in the Field and Who Have Taken the Positions to Which They Been Respectfully Appointed." Richmond, VA, January 1864.

Find a Grave | findagrave.com

Library of Congress, Prints and Photographs Division, Digital Collections, Washington, D.C.

National Archives. *Compiled Service Records of Confederate General and Staff Officers, and Nonregimental Enlisted Men.*

———. *Compiled Service Records of Confederate Soldiers Who Served in Organizations from the State of South Carolina.*

———. *Compiled Service Records of Confederate Soldiers Who Served in Organizations from the State of Virginia.*

———. *Confederate Papers Relating to Citizens or Business Firms, 1861–1865.*

NavSource Naval History | https://www.navsource.org/archives/

Navy History and Heritage Command | https:// www.history.navy.mil

Official Records of the Union and Confederate Navies. 30 vols. Washington, D.C.: U.S. Government Printing Office, 1894–1922.

Organization of Camps in the United Confederate Veterans, issues from 1896 through 1921.

South Carolina Department of Archives and History, Columbia, South Carolina.

South Caroliniana Library, University of South Carolina, Columbia, South Carolina.

Southern Historical Papers, 52 volumes. Southern Historical Society (Vols. 1–49) and the Virginia Historical Society (Vols. 50–52). Richmond, VA: 1876–1905.

Waring Historical Library, Medical University of South Carolina, Charleston, South Carolina.

The War of the Rebellion: A Compilation of the Official records of Union and Confederate Armies, 128 vols. Washington D.C.: U.S. Government Printing Office, 1880–1891.

Newspapers

Courier (Charleston, SC)
Daily Dispatch (Richmond, VA)
Daily News (Charleston, SC)
Daily Phoenix (Columbia, SC)
Evening Post (Charleston, SC)
Fairfield Journal (Winnsboro, SC)
Mercury (Charleston, SC)
News and Courier (Charleston, SC)
State (Columbia, SC)
Tarboro Southerner (Tarboro, NC)
Wilmington Journal (Wilmington, NC)

INDEX

ABOUT THE AUTHOR

D. Michael Thomas holds a BA in history from The Citadel and is a U.S. Navy veteran of the Vietnam Conflict. He coached and umpired Little League baseball for thirteen years and spent seven years as a Civil War reenactor. Michael is a longtime active member of both the American Legion and the Sons of Confederate Veterans. His previous works are *Wade Hampton's Iron Scouts: Confederate Special Forces* (2018) and *Confederate General Stephen Elliott: Beaufort Legend, Charleston Hero* (2020). He is now retired from the field of international trade.

Visit us at
www.historypress.com
....